FIRST TO A MILLION WORKBOOK

First to a Million Workbook: A Companion Guide for Teens to Achieve Early Financial Independence

Dan Sheeks

Published by BiggerPockets Publishing LLC, Denver, CO

Copyright © 2021 by Dan Sheeks

All Rights Reserved.

Publisher's Cataloging-in-Publication data

Names: Sheeks, Dan, author.

Title: First to a million workbook : a companion guide for teens to achieve early financial independence / by Dan Sheeks.

Description: Denver, CO: BiggerPockets Publishing, 2021.

Identifiers: ISBN: 9781947200630 (paperback)

Subjects: LCSH Teenagers--Finance, Personal--Handbooks, manuals, etc. | Investments--Handbooks, manuals, etc. | BISAC YOUNG ADULT NONFICTION / Activity Books | YOUNG ADULT NONFICTION / Business & Economics | YOUNG ADULT NONFICTION / Inspirational & Personal Growth | YOUNG ADULT NONFICTION / Personal Finance

Classification: LCC HG4527 .S54 2021 | DDC 332.63/22/0835--dc23

Published in the United States of America

10 9 8 7 6 5 4 3 2 1

Printed in Canada

FIRST TO A MILLION

WORKBOOK

BY DAN SHEEKS

BiggerPockets®
PUBLISHING
Denver, Colorado

TABLE OF CONTENTS

INTRODUCTION

Make no mistake about it: This book is not about money. It is about freedom, choices, opportunities, and—most of all—happiness.

—FROM *FIRST TO A MILLION*

Welcome to the First to a Million workbook!

This workbook further explains and organizes the critical strategies and concepts presented in *First to a Million* to guide you on your quest for early financial independence.

The workbook will walk you through dozens of critical action steps, including reading other books, finding a mentor, opening a brokerage account, and hitting a savings goal. The tasks are organized into four-month-long Freak Phases, which span nearly five years of your upcoming journey.

Now that you have this workbook, it's time to start working toward your FI Freak goals. Let's get going!

Your Happiness List

In Chapter Four of *First to a Million,* you created your happiness list. These list items are the ten things that bring you the most happiness. Most likely these are not "things" at all, but people you care about and experiences you share with them, most of which don't require a lot of money to enjoy. To make sure your happiness list is always close by, copy your list here. Feel free to update your list as you write it.

MY Happiness LIST

1. _____

2. _____

3. _____

4. _____

5. _____

6. _____

7. _____

8. _____

9. _____

10. _____

Your Why of FI

In Chapter Six of *First to a Million,* you created your Why of FI list. This includes the reasons and motivations you have for pursuing early FI. You then broke these down into lower-level and higher-level whys. You must review your list often to stay focused on why you live a Freakish life. The journey will not always be easy, but when things get tough, your Why of FI list will help you.

You may have put your list in a phone note or a Google Doc. To make sure your Why of FI list is always close, copy your list here. Feel free to update your list as you write it below.

My WHY of FI List

Higher-Level Whys

....

....

....

....

....

....

....

....

....

....

Lower-Level Whys

....

....

....

....

....

....

....

....

....

....

Be Flexible

While I hope this workbook becomes the bedrock of your path to early FI, it does not contain *all* the answers. Every FI Freak will have different circumstances and situations that cannot be covered in one document. Therefore, please use the First to a Million workbook as a guide and not a doctrine. You can change your course at any time and in any way, depending on your circumstances, beliefs, intentions, and ambitions.

This workbook is not a five-year plan or a ten-year plan—it is a flexible plan. Your immediate future has a lot of question marks, so don't set a goal of reaching FI by a certain age. Know that your journey will have twists and turns not accounted for in the workbook, and that's okay. Just stay focused on the goal of achieving FI, and the freedom that comes with it, at a young age.

While Freak Phase 1 is meant to be completed during the summer before your junior year of high school, you might not be in that exact place right now. *The workbook will work for you no matter where you are in life, whether in middle school or already graduated from high school.*

If you are beginning the First to a Million workbook sometime earlier than the summer before your junior year in high school, you can start completing some of the tasks in the first few Phases early. Then you can begin working each Phase as intended the summer before your junior year. If you are past the summer before your junior year of high school, you can play catch-up until you are on track. You'll still reach FI decades before most people!

You can work through the workbook faster or slower than outlined—simply modify it as needed for your situation.

Post-High School Plans

The most significant variable among FI Freaks is what they decide to do after high school. Some of you will decide to pursue a four-year degree, some of you will begin working full-time as soon as you graduate, and others will choose an option somewhere in between.

There is no right or wrong choice, but we should recognize the effect this choice will have on your ability to complete some of the tasks laid out in this workbook. Those who are going to school full-time will have less time to accomplish the First to a Million workbook tasks. In choosing to be a full-time student after high school, you have already factored in the disadvantage of having less time to actively pursue early FI. That's fine, but just remember that with your schedule, the Phases may take longer than four months to complete.

A Review of Your Freakishness

1. A person who has withdrawn from normal behavior and activities to pursue one interest or obsession.

2. One who is markedly exceptional or extraordinary.

1. A young person obsessed with making intelligent money decisions to allow themselves to reach early financial independence and live their best life.

Being a FI Freak is not a typical choice among young people. If you are young and you think about your financial future, you *are* Freakish. Only a small percentage of young people do so, which makes you extraordinary and different. Accept it, appreciate it, and capitalize on it. Very few people your age know that being Freakish about their money is actually a good thing—a very good thing, indeed.

It is *not* normal to achieve FI decades before everyone else. It is incredibly extraordinary. It is downright Freakish. So be unique. Be a FI Freak!

A Review of the Essentials

The main goal of *First to a Million* and the First to a Million workbook is to help you reach early FI. So let's take a quick look at the FI Equation:

$$Passive\ Income + Sustainable\ Asset\ Withdrawal > Living\ Expenses$$

This simple equation is the determining factor for whether you are financially independent. Always keep it in the back of your mind as you complete the workbook tasks.

In *First to a Million,* I also went over the Four Mechanisms of Early FI and how to use them in Chapters Fifteen through Twenty-Five. Just as a reminder, they are:

1. **Earn more.**
2. **Spend less.**
3. **Save the difference.**
4. **Invest your savings wisely.**

These Four Mechanisms are the tools that allow you to satisfy the FI Equation and free up decades of your future time. As you work through the tasks in each Freak Phase, I will point out when a task is helping you with a particular Mechanism.

Don't Forget to Enjoy the Journey

If I was to do it over, I wouldn't have just rushed to FI. I would have instead just thought of it as mastering my relationship between time, money, and happiness.

BRANDON GANCH, ALSO KNOWN AS THE MAD FIENTIST, ON THE *CHOOSEFI* PODCAST, EPISODE 288

Sacrificing happiness during your journey to FI goes against all the reasons for pursuing FI in the first place. As you pursue your end goal, don't forget to live in the present. If you don't keep a healthy balance in your life, your motivation and ambition will slowly fade away and you'll likely give up on your journey before reaching your goal.

Think of it this way: If you went full steam ahead toward early FI and achieved your goal in just a few years but sacrificed your happiness along the way, would that have been worthwhile? I doubt it. Instead, ease up on the gas a little bit. You might take a couple of extra years to reach FI, but preserving your happiness during the journey is worthwhile. Trust me. It's not a race; it's a journey.

Take It One Freak Phase at a Time

Some of you may feel excited about starting your journey through the First to a Million workbook. Others may feel overwhelmed. If you're in the latter group, do not fret. After you finish reading this introduction, you'll start by attacking one Freak Phase at a time.

At the beginning of each Phase, there is a list of tasks to complete. I recommend you read through the entire Freak Phase first and then come up with a plan for completing the Phase in the four-month period. When you first review the list of tasks for a given Phase, you may think there's too much to do, but remember—you have four months, which is plenty of time! Create a well-thought-out plan at the beginning of each Phase, and you'll have no problem completing all the tasks.

Tools in the Workbook

There are two tools that this workbook will use to help you complete your FI journey. You'll remember one from *First to a Million:* Freak Speak is back! Plus, I've added another tool to help you succeed.

 FREAK SPEAK: Terms that are important to understand on your FI Freak journey.

 FREAK TECHNIQUES: Strategies and tactics that are useful on your FI Freak journey.

Calendars

There will be several tasks throughout the workbook that involve putting reminders for recurring tasks in a personal calendar. To maximize your chances of achieving early FI, you should get into the habit of putting all your appointments, meetings, and tasks into a digital calendar. Then look at your calendar at least once a day, or set notifications for your events. You can use an Outlook calendar, a Google calendar, the calendar on your phone, or a calendar app.

Whatever method you choose, know that I will be referring to your "calendar" when I suggest putting an event, task, or reminder in your chosen calendar system.

Self-Education

The single most powerful asset we all have is our mind. If it is trained well, it can create enormous wealth.

—ROBERT KIYOSAKI, *RICH DAD POOR DAD*

There is no way I could include all the information you would ever need in one workbook. Therefore, to succeed on your path to early FI, you'll need to become a devoted self-educator by seeking additional information. Luckily for you, in today's world there is an infinite number of resources for all topics related to early FI.

Each Freak Phase will include a book to read to further your financial education. I have borrowed ideas from various books in this workbook, but there is obviously much more detail on the relevant strategies and concepts in the books I've borrowed from.

In addition to reading books, I will also task you with listening to podcasts and reading blog posts. These two resources will be crucial to your success. Just remember that these resources are usually meant for more experienced adults, so it's okay if you don't understand everything discussed. Do the best you can to digest the information, but you don't have to become an expert on every topic.

If you are a bookworm and want even more recommendations than are listed in this workbook, you can find a reading list at www.biggerpockets.com/teenworkbook.

Podcasts
Podcasts are a popular information source in the FIRE (Financial Independence, Retire Early) and REI (real estate investing) communities. To be a genuine FI Freak, you should find two or three podcasts and become a devoted listener of each. There is a wide variety of podcasts covering a broad range of topics, and most are free to download. Generally, a podcaster will publish new episodes regularly, such as every Monday, meaning podcasts are a veritable fountain of new information.

Here is the first recurring reminder to put in your calendar: **Start listening to at least three podcast episodes per week.** Since this task is a frequent one, you might use your recurring calendar reminder only until you get into the habit of listening to at least three episodes a week.

- **Tip:** Browse through the titles of the first fifty episodes of any podcast, as most hosts start their podcasts with more basic introductory episodes.
- **Tip:** Listen to podcasts (and audiobooks) while driving, exercising, or doing chores.
- **Tip:** When you listen to podcasts, you can change the speed of the recording. I recommend listening to episodes at 1.5x speed.

For a list of some great podcast shows and episodes, go to biggerpockets.com/teenworkbook.

Blog Posts
Blogs are another favorite resource of the FIRE and REI communities. Many people have documented their journeys toward early FI and investing through personal blogs. Engaging with blogs and reading

articles that pique your interest is a fantastic way to educate yourself.

Now it's time for your second recurring calendar reminder: **Start reading at least three blog posts per week.** Find your own favorite blog sites by searching for subjects and topics that are interesting to you.

- **Tip:** Just as with podcasts, it can be beneficial to browse the titles of the earliest posts on a blog, since they are likely more basic.

For a list of some great blogs and posts, go to biggerpockets.com/teenworkbook.

Sharing Your Journey

As you enter Freak Phase 1, consider documenting your experiences as you follow your path to early FI. When you reflect on your wins and losses, you'll deepen your commitment and learn more in the process. By sharing those experiences, you can help others learn from your journey too!

There will be many other FI Freaks working their way through their own First to a Million workbook. Connecting with these people will help you find strength, encouragement, friendship, and inspiration. The journey to early FI is not one you should take alone. If you walk this path with other FI Freaks, your journey will be easier and your victory much more meaningful.

Here are some ways to share with other FI Freaks. Pick the ones you like best, and put recurring reminders in your calendar to check in with your Freakish friends.

- Make short videos or take pictures and post them on your social media accounts. Use the hashtag #teenagefifreak, and don't forget to tag @biggerpockets and @sheeksfreaks!
- Write a blog post of your own (short and sweet is best). Email it to info@sheeksfreaks.com and we may feature your article in the community!
- Submit your wins and losses to the SheeksFreaks community at www.sheeksfreaks.com/submit-your-story. What milestone or big breakthrough did you recently achieve? What setback did you experience that you want others to watch out for?
- Start your own YouTube channel or blog to document your journey.
- Create a BiggerPockets profile and share your finance and investing journey with a post in the member forums.

Start *now*. Post a video about your happiness list and your Why of FI list to your social media accounts, and make sure to include the hashtags #teenagefifreak and #fifreakworkbookday1. Watch as others reach out and support you, and don't forget to comment and support others while you're there.

The journey starts now.

It's finally time to get your Freak on!

FREAK PHASE *One*

MAY–AUGUST
Summer before junior year of high school

Wealth doesn't care if you are smart, stupid, fat, skinny, tall, short, white, black, male, or female… It doesn't matter if you are "better" or "worse" than someone else. Wealth is simply a function of knowledge, action and time… The principles of wealth are well within the grasp of every human that has the capacity to learn.

—SCOTT TRENCH, "INCOME INEQUALITY: ARE THE WEALTHY SUPERIOR PEOPLE OR IS THE SYSTEM UNFAIR?,"
BIGGERPOCKETS BLOG

Here is the checklist for this four-month Freak Phase. It's best to read the entire Freak Phase *before* filling in the due date for each item. This is because some of the task descriptions will include sections for you to write down notes, goals, checkpoints, variations, action steps, and more. Filling in those sections first will aid you in coming up with appropriate due dates. Don't forget to use your calendar to help you stay on track. Once you complete a task, check it off in the right column. You're a FI Freak, so you've got this! Best of luck!

DUE DATES	✓	TASK
	○	Read *First to a Million* by Dan Sheeks.
	○	Read *Personal Finance for Teens* by Carol H. Cox.
	○	Set three financial goals.
	○	Implement a new Freak Tweak.
	○	Sell a personal item you no longer need or want.
	○	Find and do a new fun, free activity.
	○	Go over the household bills with a parent every month.
	○	Register for beneficial classes during your junior year.
	○	Have a parent add you as an authorized user on their credit card.
	○	Have a parent help you open a checking account.
	○	Start tracking your income and expenses.
	○	Get a job.
	○	Create goal-oriented social media accounts.

Read *First to a Million*

I assume you found this workbook because you've read *First to a Million*. If that is not the case, read that book before you do anything else.

Read *Personal Finance for Teens*

Sometimes learning about personal finance topics can be less than thrilling, but this book provides vital information for your FI journey. Although it may be a bit dry in places, you should at least read the chapters recommended below—without them, you might have difficulty following this workbook.

Keep in mind that almost every personal finance book presents information based on the assumption that you are satisfied with the idea of working until you are 65 years old (or older), and *Personal Finance for Teens* is no different. However, because you are a FI Freak and not the average young person, some chapters in this book do not apply to you.

Here are my recommendations:

CHAPTER CHECKLIST FOR
PERSONAL FINANCE FOR TEENS:

- ☐ **Chapter 1:** Managing a Checking Account
- ☐ **Chapter 2:** Getting a Job (optional depending on your situation)
- ☐ **Chapter 3:** Understanding Taxes and Your Paycheck
- ☐ **Chapter 4:** Creating a Spending Plan
- ☐ **Chapter 5:** Understanding How Credit Scores Work
- ☐ **Chapter 6:** Using Credit Cards Intelligently
- ☐ **Chapter 7:** Making College More Affordable
- ☐ **Chapter 8:** What a Car Really Costs

Chapter One explains how to manage a checking account effectively. If you don't currently have a checking account, read this chapter before getting one (which is one of the other tasks in this Freak Phase). It is vital to keep track of your checking account balance and transactions. The book talks about using a "check register" or "transaction register," which is a written log of all your transactions, to do so. You could also use a Google Sheet or an Excel spreadsheet.

One of the other tasks you'll be completing in this Freak Phase is to start tracking all your income and expenses. Doing this will be much simpler if you have a solid understanding of managing the money in your checking account.

Set Three Financial Goals

Setting goals is the first step in turning the invisible into the visible.

—TONY ROBBINS

FT **SETTING GOALS:** Setting tangible and achievable goals is a common habit among successful people and has been proven effective in numerous studies.

You'll be doing this task at the beginning of every Freak Phase. Focus on objectives *not* included in that Phase's checklist. Everyone's path to early FI is a little different. You can add critical goals that are particular to your personal journey.

When you set a goal, it should have these four traits:

- It should be specific.
- It should be measurable.
- It should be achievable.
- It should have a time frame.

Here are some examples:

I will save $1,800 for an electric scooter next year by saving $150 from each month's paycheck for one year. *By the end of this summer (August 31st), I will have started my first side hustle and made $500 in revenue.* *Within the next sixty days, I will watch twenty hours of YouTube videos about entrepreneurship for teenagers.*

Accountability Partner

FREAK SPEAK

 FS **ACCOUNTABILITY PARTNER:** A person who coaches or supports another person in keeping a commitment.

To help you achieve your goals, you'll need an accountability partner who understands how important those goals are to you. The job of an accountability partner is to encourage and support the goal seeker, check in and see how things are going, and call out the goal seeker when they are not working hard to achieve their goals. It is important that the accountability partner hold the goal seeker accountable, rather than consoling or coddling them when they are not progressing as they hoped.

Once you have chosen your accountability partner and explained what you would like them to do, you'll need to communicate your goals to them at the beginning of each Freak Phase.

✚ Put a **RECURRING REMINDER** in your calendar to complete this task at the beginning of every Freak Phase.

Goals

+ ACTION STEPS

Write out your three goals for this Freak Phase here.

Put any necessary reminders in your calendar so you can reach these goals.

1 ....

2 ....

3 ....

DATE: _____

The date I communicated my three goals to my accountability partner.

Implement a New Freak Tweak
Being frugal is the cornerstone of wealth-building.

—THOMAS J. STANLEY AND WILLIAM D. DANKO, *THE MILLIONAIRE NEXT DOOR*

Chapter Seventeen in *First to a Million* discusses the importance of frugality and some specific ways you can be more frugal. Frugality is essential for maximizing the potential of Mechanism 2, *spend less*.

Remember: Frugality is *not* about deprivation or sacrifice. Frugality is simply about being intentional with how you spend your money. It is about giving thought to your purchases (even the small ones) to determine if they will bring you joy and satisfaction.

These decisions depend on your personal values. If a potential purchase is something that will bring you great delight and happiness, you should absolutely spend the money on it. But if the potential purchase will bring you little to no value, then pass on it and save the money to fuel your FI journey.

What will you get from making these frugal choices? You'll get early FI. You'll get decades of freedom. Saving more money with frugality decreases your living expenses, making the FI Equation easier to reach:

$$Passive\ Income + Sustainable\ Asset\ Withdrawal > Living\ Expenses$$

For each Freak Phase you'll implement one new way to apply frugality in your life. A creative way to be frugal is known as a "Freak Tweak." If at any time you find it challenging to come up with an idea, simply Google "frugality ideas" or refer to Chapter Seventeen in *First to a Million*. (By the way, feel free to list more than one new idea!) Depending on which Freak Tweak you have chosen, it may help to put a reminder in your calendar.

My New FREAK Tweak FOR FRUGALITY IS...

....

....

....

....

....

....

....

+ Put a **RECURRING REMINDER** in your calendar to complete
+ this task at the beginning of every Freak Phase.

Sell a Personal Item You No Longer Need or Want

You probably own some items that you no longer need or want. They could be items you have outgrown or no longer value.

 SELLING UNWANTED BELONGINGS: A strategy that declutters your life and increases income.

Think back to the happiness curve from Chapter Five in *First to a Million*. The curve shows that there is a point at which we have "enough." After we reach the point of enough, which includes necessities and some luxury items, our happiness level is maxed out. Decluttering our lives helps us to stay at or near the point of enough so we maximize our happiness. It also utilizes Mechanism 1, *earn more*.

An item that has a small monetary value could be a waste of time to sell. For example, if you want to sell a hoodie that's worth $10 but you spend a total of two hours dealing with all the aspects of selling it, you will have made $5 an hour. That's not a good use of your time. Instead, consider donating inexpensive items to a local charity or secondhand store.

If the value of the unwanted item is $50 or more, there are many platforms you can use to sell it. I suggest trying one at a time to see which has the most success in your area. Some possible platforms are:

- eBay (best for big-ticket items)
- Craigslist (best for selling locally, but beware of scammers!)
- Facebook Marketplace (best for selling locally, with fewer scammers than Craigslist)
- OfferUp
- Nextdoor
- Letgo

MAKE A LIST OF ITEMS WORTH AT LEAST

$50

THAT YOU COULD SELL:

The Item I Will Sell During This Freak Phase Is:

+ Put a **RECURRING REMINDER** in your calendar to complete this task every Freak Phase. Refer back to this list for ideas on what to sell.

Find and Do a New Fun, Free Activity

Nothing matters in life more than great moments with people we care about in places we love to be.

—GENE NATALI ON THE *NGPF PODCAST*

Part of living a frugal life is finding ways to add happiness with little or no cost. It's okay to spend money doing things you love with the people you cherish, but it's also a good idea to periodically try some low-cost or free activities with those same people. This is another nifty way to apply Mechanism 2, *spend less.*

ENGAGING IN FREE ACTIVITIES: By finding free ways to entertain yourself, you are hammering Mechanism 2 and will reach FI faster.

Instead of going out to eat with your best friend, try packing a lunch and having a picnic with them in your local park. Or instead of going skiing on your day off from school or work, rent some snowshoes (much cheaper!), explore a free trail, and bring some snacks in a backpack.

Here are some other free or low-cost activities that could add happiness without subtracting from your FI goals.

- Do a geocaching scavenger hunt.
- Read a book.
- Host a movie marathon.

- Bake something you've never made before.
- Play a board game with your family or friends.
- Spend time outdoors hiking, biking, or gardening.
- Host a potluck dinner with your favorite people.
- Have a campfire in your backyard and make s'mores with your friends.
- Talk a stroll in your city's downtown.
- Go to the beach.
- Take a free class online.
- Visit garage sales with your best friend and look for deals.

LIST SOME MORE FREE OR LOW-COST ACTIVITIES YOU WOULD FIND FUN:

The new *Fun and Free* ACTIVITY I will do during this Freak Phase is:

✚ Put a **RECURRING REMINDER** in your calendar to complete this task at the beginning of every Freak Phase. Refer back to this list for ideas.

Go Over the Household Bills with a Parent Every Month

The best way to learn about managing money is to be involved with the process. You probably wouldn't consider participating in your parent's monthly ritual of paying the family bills as prime quality time, but it is a Freakishly magnificent learning opportunity. The chance to get insight into the income and expenses of the small business known as your family is one you should not pass up.

 HELPING WITH MONTHLY HOUSEHOLD BILLS: By helping a parent organize and pay the household bills, you are learning about the financial responsibilities of an adult.

If you're lucky enough to have a financially savvy parent, use them as a resource for maximizing your financial future. Otherwise, maybe you could teach them a thing or two.

To gain a better understanding of money, ask a parent:

- If you can observe them while they pay bills.
- If they can go over the household's monthly income and expenses.
- If they will let you help them balance their checking account.
- If you can watch them while they invest their money.
- If they will go over their paystub with you.
- Why money goes *here* and not *there*.
- If they are able to do something to earn more income. (Mechanism 1)
- What they do to spend less. (Mechanism 2)
- What their savings rate is. (Mechanism 3)
- How their investments are doing. (Mechanism 4)
- If they will explain their employer's 401(k) match to you.
- What they would do if they won $10,000, $100,000, or $1 million.

If your parent is willing to discuss some or all of these things with you, a useful conversation about your family's finances will follow. You can learn a ton just from what your parent is doing (or not doing) with their money. These conversations can happen at the nightly dinner table or while riding in the car, walking the dog, making breakfast on a weekend morning, or browsing the grocery store aisle. Anytime you're with them, you can ask questions.

 Put a **RECURRING REMINDER** in your calendar to complete this task every month.

Use This Space to Take Notes on Household Budgeting

Register for Beneficial Classes During Junior Year

If you are reading this during summer vacation, it may be a bit late to decide what classes you'll take next year. But even if you have already registered, you should make a list of classes that can help you achieve your early FI goal. You might be able to change a class or two once you get back to school, or you could tweak your schedule for the second semester next year. At the very least, you will have a better idea of which classes you'll want to take during your senior year.

As explained in Chapter Twenty-Six of *First to a Million*, there are several classes your high school may offer that can boost your FI journey. And they're free! Here are a few:

- Personal finance
- Computer applications (or another class that teaches how to use Excel)
- Accounting
- Entrepreneurship
- Marketing
- Video editing (helpful with certain side hustles)
- Classes that offer concurrent enrollment or dual enrollment (you receive college credit)

If you need to put a reminder in your calendar to talk to your school counselor or registrar as soon as you return to school this fall, do it now. Otherwise, look over your school's course guide and make a list of classes you would like to add, swap, or take before you graduate from high school.

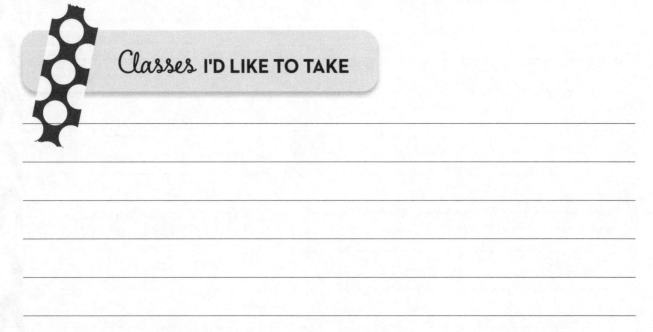

Classes I'D LIKE TO TAKE

Ask a Parent to Add You as an Authorized User on Their Credit Card

In Chapters Eleven and Twelve of *First to Million*, we went over the crucial importance of building your credit score and how credit cards can help you do that.

You are not legally allowed to get a credit card until you are 18, but there is a workaround. If your parent has a credit card, they can likely add you to the account as an "authorized user." As an authorized user, you are not ultimately responsible for the money charged on the credit card, but your parent is allowing you to use the credit card to make purchases. When your parent pays off the balance every month (the responsible way to use a credit card), it can have a positive effect on their credit score *and* yours. Becoming an authorized user on your parent's credit card allows you to start building an excellent credit score before you are 18.

 AUTHORIZED USER: An additional cardholder on someone else's credit card account who receives a credit card in their name that is linked to the primary cardholder's account.

You'll need your parent's permission, but if you can prove to them you understand the negative consequences of using a credit card recklessly and can convince them you won't do so, they should be willing to add you.

Use this checklist to track your progress on becoming an authorized user. ➡

Ask a Parent to Help You Open a Checking Account

In Chapter Twenty of *First to a Million*, you learned that money in your checking account should be for regular expenses like paying your bills and conducting your everyday life. Chapter One in *Personal Finance for Teens* covers checking accounts in depth.

Checking accounts are the most basic accounts offered by banks, and they have many advantages:

- Checking accounts can be free, especially for students.
- You can lose cash, but you can't lose money in a checking account.
- Pretty much every checking account will have a debit card, which you can use to make purchases or get cash from an ATM.

 TO DO:

Ask parent if they will allow you to become an authorized user on their account.

 Ask parent about their credit score and how often they make credit card payments. (If your parent is irresponsible with their credit cards, don't become an authorized user on their account!)

Have parent call the credit card company to inquire about adding you as an authorized user. (Sometimes there are restrictions.)

Have parent make sure the company will also report on-time payments to your credit history. (Sometimes they won't—even if you're an authorized user.)

 Receive your credit card. (It can take a few weeks to arrive in the mail.)

- Just about every bank has an app that will allow you to quickly check your balance, look at recent transactions, transfer money to a friend, and find ATMs or bank locations nearby.
- You can set up some bills to automatically deduct from your checking account, and you can pay other bills directly from the app on your phone.
- You can have your paycheck deposited directly into your checking account.

The younger you are when you open your first checking account, the better—but since you are under 18, a parent will have to open the account with you. Their name will also be on the account as a "joint account holder," but it will be *your* money in *your* account. Since you are a high school student, a student checking account—which all major banks offer—is the way to go. And don't forget to download the bank's app to your phone.

Use this checklist to track your progress in opening your checking account. ⬇

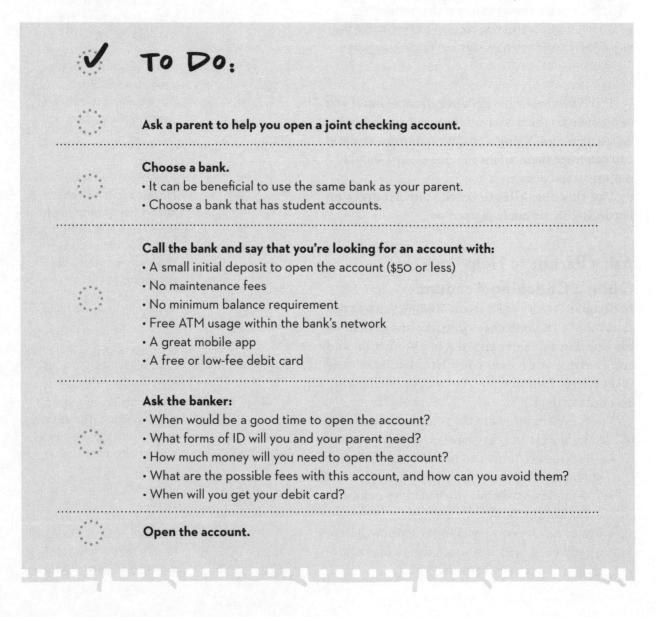

✔ **TO DO:**

○ **Ask a parent to help you open a joint checking account.**

○ **Choose a bank.**
• It can be beneficial to use the same bank as your parent.
• Choose a bank that has student accounts.

○ **Call the bank and say that you're looking for an account with:**
• A small initial deposit to open the account ($50 or less)
• No maintenance fees
• No minimum balance requirement
• Free ATM usage within the bank's network
• A great mobile app
• A free or low-fee debit card

○ **Ask the banker:**
• When would be a good time to open the account?
• What forms of ID will you and your parent need?
• How much money will you need to open the account?
• What are the possible fees with this account, and how can you avoid them?
• When will you get your debit card?

○ **Open the account.**

Start Tracking Your Income and Expenses

Chapter Nineteen in *First to a Million* covers tracking your income and expenses. If you don't remember much from that chapter, I highly suggest reviewing it before you read through this task, which is an unbelievably useful tool for maximizing Mechanism 2, *spend less*.

 TRACKING INCOME AND EXPENSES: Keeping track of all the money that comes in and goes out of your life, allowing you to set more accurate financial goals and monitor your progress toward early FI.

On your journey to early FI, you must be aware of every dollar that comes into and goes out of your life. Luckily, doing this is pretty straightforward and even a little fun! As a teenager, you probably don't have hundreds or thousands of dollars in income or expenses, but starting this habit now will allow you to adjust your systems easily as your financial responsibilities grow over time.

Many free apps can help you track your money. I recommend Mint, but there are other quality choices, such as Wally, YNAB (You Need a Budget), Personal Capital, and PocketSmith. Once you have set up your tracking account and synced all your financial accounts (checking accounts, savings accounts, investment accounts, Venmo, PayPal, etc.), every dollar you earn or spend will automatically appear in your tracking account.

Be sure to explore all of the app's options and make this your go-to place to see your overall money picture. I check my Mint app at least once a day to see what's going on. It can also tell you about upcoming bills you need to pay or large transactions you should double-check.

✓ TASK

○ Choose a tracking app and create an account.

○ Sync all your financial accounts.

○ Set up your initial expense categories. (You can add more later as needed.)

○ Put a weekly reminder in your calendar to update and categorize your recent transactions in your tracking app.

○ Put a monthly reminder in your calendar to add all cash transactions from the previous month into your tracking app.

Get a Job

Summer is here. That means no school for about three months! Yes, it's time to have some fun, but it's also time to start making (and saving) some money, aka hammer Mechanisms 1 and 2.

Without classes and homework filling your schedule, a full-time job is a definite possibility. I recommend you work somewhere forty hours per week *and* find another way to make money with a part-time job or a side hustle. Parts of your summer may be busy with family vacations or summer camp, but there is undoubtedly some extra time for you to rack up the hours and some Benjamins.

In Chapter Sixteen of *First to a Million*, I go over how a teenager can make money. Review that chapter as you begin to think about finding the best way(s) to make money this summer. It covers many options for part-time jobs, full-time jobs, and even some next-level jobs, which are great for anyone interested in REI. By working a job related to real estate, you'll be doing what Robert Kiyosaki calls "working to learn, not to earn." (Though you'll still get paid, which is a nice bonus!)

Look back at Chapter Sixteen for job ideas, find a job category that interests you, and approach as many businesses in that category as you can. If you need more guidance on applying for and getting a job, refer to Chapter Two of *Personal Finance for Teens*.

Paystubs

When you get your first paycheck, sit down with a parent and go over each line and number on the paycheck/paystub. Ask questions about what each item is. You may want to google some of the items to learn more. (As a bonus, you can ask a parent to go over *their* paystub.)

List the businesses where you'll apply for a job.

NAME OF BUSINESS	MILES FROM HOME	EXPECTED PAY RATE	APPLIED?	FOLLOWED UP?	INTERVIEWED?

Create Goal-Oriented Social Media Accounts

Social media is an important part of most of our lives. Right now, you may have two, three, four, or more social media accounts, all of which are vying for your attention and time. Let me ask you one quick question:

Who are the customers of these mega social media platforms?

If you answered "the users" or "the members," you are way off. *You* are not their customer. Not even close. The companies that pay to advertise on these social media platforms are the customers—and you are the *product*! Social media companies are actually selling access to your attention and time to advertisers.

If you feel used, don't let it get you down. There are ways to use social media that are healthy *and* can help you reach your goals, even if the social media companies don't have your best interest in mind. Start some new social media accounts strictly for building your network and marketing your skills and abilities (even if you haven't acquired them yet). Choose a username that is professional. In your bio, put "aspiring real estate investor" or "financial freedom freak." Let your tagline or bio speak about who you really are (a FI Freak) and what goals you have.

 PROFESSIONAL SOCIAL MEDIA ACCOUNTS: Social media accounts designed to network and promote yourself on your FI Freak journey.

Switch your mindset from "look at all the stuff I have and cool things I do" to "look at how I'm frugal, saving for my future, and learning new skills." Instead of posting pictures and updates on social media about a new item or experience that cost you hundreds of dollars, post something you did that *saved* you hundreds of dollars. That's what a Freak would do.

Don't go overboard creating new accounts—if you do, you'll spend too much of your valuable time monitoring and updating them. Choose one or two platforms and keep your accounts current by posting once or twice a week. As you progress on your journey to financial freedom, people will notice your Freakish choices and see how they are paying off.

At first, they will ask, "Why are they doing that?"

Later, they will look at your social media posts and ask, "*How* did they do that?"

The following are just some of the hashtags you can use to find visibility:

#frugalfreak	#realestateinvestor	#financialindependence
#sidehustle	#stockinvestingiscool	#freedom
#financiallyliterate	#paymyselffirst	#getyourfreakon

Choose one or two platforms for your new accounts and fill in this chart.

SOCIAL MEDIA PLATFORM(S)	USERNAME	BIO/TAGLINE	FIRST POST WILL BE

✚ Put a **RECURRING REMINDER** in your calendar to post something to your new
Freakish social media account(s) once or twice a week.

Congratulations! You've just completed Freak Phase 1! It's time to be proud of your Freakishness and check in with your progress. Post a video of yourself describing the three most meaningful tasks you completed in this Freak Phase, and post a picture of yourself with your completed checklist from the beginning of this Phase. Don't forget to use **#FREAKPHASE1** and **#TEENAGEFIFREAK** and to tag **@SHEEKSFREAKS** and **@BIGGERPOCKETS!**

FREAK PHASE *Two*

SEPTEMBER–DECEMBER
First semester of junior year of high school

I found that nothing in life is worthwhile unless you take risks. Nothing . . . You will fail at some point in your life. Accept it. You will lose. You will embarrass yourself. You will suck at something. There's no doubt about it . . . Embrace it because it's inevitable . . . To get something you never had, you have to do something you never did.

—DENZEL WASHINGTON

Here is the checklist for this four-month Freak Phase. It's best to read the entire Freak Phase before filling in the due date for each item. Don't forget to use your calendar to help you stay on track. And remember—you're a FI Freak, so you've got this!

DUE DATES	✓	TASK
	○	Read *Rich Dad Poor Dad* by Robert Kiyosaki.
	○	Have a parent help you open a savings account.
	○	Create free accounts on LinkedIn, BiggerPockets, and SheeksFreaks.
	○	Start networking.
	○	Interview someone who is where you want to be.
	○	Balance your checking and savings accounts every month.
	○	Calculate and track your net worth.
	○	Pay yourself first—at least 30 percent of your income.
	○	Calculate and track your savings rate.
	○	Evaluate your core circle.
	○	Start a side hustle.
	○	Set three financial goals.
	○	Implement a new Freak Tweak.
	○	Sell a personal item you no longer need or want.
	○	Find and do a new fun, free activity.

Write out your three goals for this Freak Phase here.

1 ....

2 ....

3 ....

DATE: _____

The date I communicated my three goals to my accountability partner.

My New FREAK Tweak FOR FRUGALITY IS...

....

....

....

....

....

....

....

....

....

....

....

....

Put a **RECURRING REMINDER** in your calendar to complete these tasks at the beginning of every Freak Phase.

Read *Rich Dad Poor Dad*

This book by Robert Kiyosaki is considered a must-read by many in the FIRE and REI communities. It's a great introduction to the mindset one needs to build wealth, attain passive income streams, and reach early FI.

Have a Parent Help You Open a Savings Account

Let's get to work on Mechanism 3! Since you are not 18 yet, a parent will have to help you open a savings account. Just like your checking account, this will be a joint account, with both your parent and you listed on the account. If you already have a savings account, great! If not, tell your parent you would like to open one to start saving money for your future.

If they don't help you, you'll have to wait until you're 18 and leave all your "saved" money in your checking account. If you don't have either a checking or a savings account, then you may ask a trusted adult to keep your money in a bank account for you, or keep your cash in a small safe at home.

In Chapter Twenty of *First to a Million*, we learned that your checking account's money should be for regular expenses, but a savings account is for saving. We also went over the many benefits of a savings account. For more information about opening a savings account, you can refer back to Chapter Twenty, as well as to the blog post linked at biggerpockets.com/teenworkbook.

If you already have a checking account, I recommend opening your savings account at the same bank or credit union. Eventually, you'll want to have three savings accounts, but for now, one account is fine for all your saved money. It's better to wait until you're 18 to open those two other savings accounts, and the workbook will remind you to do just that.

Use this checklist to track your progress in opening your savings account.

✔ TO DO:

○ Ask a parent to help you open a joint savings account.

○ Choose a bank.

○ Call the bank and say that you're interested in opening a savings account with your parent.

○ Ask the banker:
  - What is the interest rate on the savings account?
  - When would be a good time to open the account?
  - What forms of ID will you and your parent need?
  - How much money will you need to open the account?
  - What are the possible fees with this account, and how can you avoid them?

○ Open the account.

Create Free Accounts on LinkedIn, BiggerPockets, and SheeksFreaks

LinkedIn

LinkedIn is the world's largest social media platform for professional networking. As you forge ahead on your path to early FI, networking on LinkedIn will become more and more important. But it is much different from the social media platforms you may be used to.

First off, there are very few photos. You'll have a profile picture of yourself (it should look very professional), and that's it. Yes, you read that correctly: You'll post only one picture of yourself. The rest of your profile consists of information regarding your experiences, your goals, your education, and other similar aspects of your professional life.

Make sure your headline and "about" section match that of the goal-oriented social media accounts you set up in the last Phase. It should include something like "aspiring real estate investor" or "financial freedom freak." Once you've created the account, spend some time entering information about yourself. You can enter information such as:

- An introduction about yourself (highly recommended)
- Background information
- Work and volunteer experience
- Special skills
- Accomplishments

Next, find and connect with as many people as you can. These people may include past and present teachers, past and present classmates, adult friends, relatives, and anyone else you know.

Do these three things to complete this task:

BiggerPockets

If you haven't created a BiggerPockets membership account yet, now's the time to do just that. The basic level of membership is free, and for now, that is all you need. Go to www.biggerpockets.com to create your free account. Also, download the free app.

BiggerPockets is a unique online community for real estate investors. But it's much more than that. It's the best place to go for everything you could want to know about REI and related topics. There's information on investing, money management, side hustles, saving money, and more. In fact, the website has so many resources that it can be overwhelming until you become familiar with everything available. To begin, try focusing on one resource at a time.

First, go into the forums (www.biggerpockets.com/forums) and look around. If you post a question on a forum, you'll probably get responses before the end of the day. Connect with those who respond and always thank them for their input. You'll find that BP members are more than happy to help young people and will see your determination as quite impressive (which it is!).

 ONLINE FORUMS: Discussion sites where people can hold conversations in the form of posted messages.

Next, explore the blog posts (www.biggerpockets.com/blog), where you'll find numerous articles about a wide variety of topics. Search for those you are learning about or are interested in.

Other great resources on the BiggerPockets website include a glossary, free webinars, podcast episodes, and calculators. Also, don't forget to check out the BiggerPockets YouTube channel (www.youtube.com/user/BiggerPockets) and bookstore (www.biggerpockets.com/store).

Do these three things to complete this task:

POST A QUESTION
IN A BIGGERPOCKETS FORUM. KEEP AN EYE ON YOUR POST FOR THE FIRST FORTY-EIGHT HOURS AND RESPOND TO ANY REPLIES OR COMMENTS YOU RECEIVE.

READ A BLOG POST
THAT HAS ONE OF THESE TERMS IN THE TITLE: "YOUNG," "TEEN," "TEENAGER," OR "HIGH SCHOOL."

WATCH
A BIGGERPOCKETS YOUTUBE VIDEO AND SUBSCRIBE.

SheeksFreaks

SheeksFreaks (www.sheeksfreaks.com) is the only online community specifically for people just like you. It is a group of Freakish young people who are highly motivated to learn and find success in entrepreneurship, investing, real estate, money management, and early FI. Most members are between 15 and 25 years old.

The website has many resources specifically for young Freaks, such as blog posts, a resources page, Featured Freak submissions, a video gallery, and success stories. Membership is free, and all are welcome.

The SheeksFreaks community is also on:

 @sheeksfreaks   SheeksFreaks   @sheeksfreaks

Do these three things to complete this task:

CREATE AN ACCOUNT ON THE

SHEEKSFREAKS WEBSITE.

SUBSCRIBE TO THE SHEEKSFREAKS YOUTUBE CHANNEL AND FOLLOW SHEEKSFREAKS ON INSTAGRAM AND TIKTOK.

FIND A BLOG POST

THAT IS INTERESTING TO YOU, READ IT, AND COMMENT ON THE ARTICLE.

Start Networking

Your network is your net worth.

—UNKNOWN

Meeting and connecting with other people is what networking is all about. Networking allows you to find key people who can turbocharge your path to early FI. Your network will come in handy when you need help or advice or are seeking new opportunities. Starting now, the people you connect with will be crucial to your success.

FREAK TECHNIQUE

NETWORKING: Interacting with others to exchange information and develop professional or social contacts.

Education and networking are two essential parts of your journey. Most people prefer one over the other based on their personality. Introverts will lean toward education from books, podcasts, blogs, and forums. Extroverts will lean toward getting out and meeting people at events, conferences, seminars, and meetups. No matter which you favor today, you'll need to excel at both.

Networking can happen in person or remotely. Here are a few ways to meet people in person:
- Go to local meetups for groups that align with your early FI pathway. (www.meetup.com)
- Attend local events with other BiggerPockets members.
- Join your local Real Estate Investors Association (REIA) and attend some of their meetings. (www.nationalreia.org)

Here are two ways to network remotely:
- Grow your connections on LinkedIn, BiggerPockets, and SheeksFreaks by messaging a few people each week.
- Use your new social media accounts to DM influential people. When possible, send a video message instead of a text message.

When reaching out to someone, your message could be something like this:

Hello, Chase. My name is Dan Sheeks, and I'm a high school student in Colorado. I'm very interested in the investing industry, and I see you've been working for Charles Schwab for a few years. I'm wondering what your job is like. Do you enjoy it? How did you get your job? What advice would you give to someone who wants to pursue an investing career? Is there anything that you need help with? Thanks ahead of time for any advice you may have.

It's that simple. You can tweak the wording to fit your specific objective. Just remember to always be respectful and friendly. Each person you meet can change your life by presenting new opportunities. Start your lifelong networking journey now!

List some actions, events, or strategies you'll complete during each month of this Phase to build your network. Put any necessary reminders in your calendar.

MONTH 1

MONTH 2

MONTH 3

- -

- -

- -

- -

MONTH 4

- -

- -

- -

- -

Interview Someone Who Is Where You Want to Be

As you start to grow your network, create opportunities to do more than just connect. Your network will undoubtedly include people who are where you want to be on your FI Freak journey. It makes sense that you should talk to these people and ask for advice or assistance.

To complete this task, you will identify and interview one person every month who you feel has some wisdom and experience to offer you. Once you've identified these people, reach out and ask if you may interview them. Tell them you are inspired by their accomplishments and would love to know more about how they got to where they are now.

Make a list of people you can reach out to and a list of questions you'll ask during the interview. As you spend more time on your networking accounts, your list of possible interviewees will grow. Come back and add new names when this happens. For now, brainstorm at least five generic questions that you can ask anyone. For example, "What is the accomplishment you are most proud of?"

The interviews can be completed with a phone call, a video meeting (Zoom, for example), or in person. You'll be completing this task during every Phase, which means you will interview someone every month going forward.

Put a **RECURRING REMINDER** in your calendar to complete this task every Phase.

People I Would Like To Interview

1. _____   6. _____

2. _____   7. _____

3. _____   8. _____

4. _____   9. _____

5. _____   10. _____

Questions I Will Ask

_____

_____

_____

_____

_____

_____

_____

_____

_____

_____

MONTH 1 / DATE COMPLETED

....

PERSON TO INTERVIEW

....

MONTH 2 / DATE COMPLETED

....

PERSON TO INTERVIEW

....

MONTH 3 / DATE COMPLETED

....

PERSON TO INTERVIEW

....

MONTH 4 / DATE COMPLETED

....

PERSON TO INTERVIEW

....

Refer back to your list of possible interviewees in Freak Phase 2.

Balance Your Checking and Savings Accounts Every Month

Strong organizational skills translate very directly into financial empowerment and control.

—CHRIS SMITH, *I AM NET WORTHY*

Being organized with your bookkeeping and monthly bills is critical to your financial future. Start building good habits now.

Forming Good Habits

- **Habit 1:** Use only ATMs that don't charge a fee.

- **Habit 2:** Check the balance in your checking account often (at least twice a week) using the bank's app. Make sure you aren't close to overdrawing your account (going below zero) and that there are no unexpected transactions. If possible, set up text alerts that will notify you when your balance falls below a certain amount.

- **Habit 3:** If you see an unexpected fee on your monthly bank statement, call your bank and ask about it.

- **Habit 4:** Use your debit card to buy only things you need.

- **Habit 5:** Balance your checking and savings accounts every month. It's not enough to just look at your monthly bank statements, although many people don't even do that. In addition, you should go through each transaction on those bank statements and compare it to what you have in your records.

Direct Deposit Your Paycheck

If you have a job for which you receive a regular paycheck, you should set up direct deposit. To do this, talk to your boss and let them know you would like to have your paycheck direct deposited into your checking account. If they can do this, they will have a form for you to fill out that permits them to send your earnings directly to your account. The form will ask for your bank account number and your bank's routing number. You can find these under your account info on your bank's app.

USING DIRECT DEPOSIT: Having a paycheck deposited directly into your checking account.

Paying Your Bills

As a teenager, you likely have few, if any, bills for which you are responsible. If you don't have any, ask a parent if you can be responsible for paying one of your household's monthly bills—perhaps the cell phone bill or the trash collector bill. By doing this and forming solid behaviors now, you'll be well prepared to handle the multiple monthly bills you'll have as an adult.

Here are some tips to help you set up a system that makes the bill-paying process easy and reduces the chances of missing a payment.

- Have the first day of the month (give or take a day or two) be the due date for as many bills as possible. You can call each company and request they change your monthly due date.
- Have a list of all your monthly bills, their due dates, and the amount (exact or approximate) of each.
- Set up as many bills as you can to "auto-pay," which means the bill is automatically paid from your checking account each month.
- Pay all your monthly bills on the 25th of each month. This buffer of a few days between the day you pay your bills and their due date is important.
- On the day you pay your bills, begin by balancing your checking and savings accounts based on your most recent bank statements.

✛ Put a **RECURRING REMINDER** in your calendar to balance your accounts and pay your bills every month.

Calculate and Track Your Net Worth

Wealth is more often the result of a lifestyle of hard work, perseverance, planning, and, most of all, self-discipline.

—THOMAS J. STANLEY AND WILLIAM D. DANKO, *THE MILLIONAIRE NEXT DOOR*

If you track your income and expenses using an app such as Mint, calculating your net worth will be easy. For a refresher on the concept of net worth, review Chapter Thirteen in *First to a Million*, where I explain what net worth is and how to calculate it.

 CALCULATING NET WORTH: Regularly determining the total of your assets minus the total of your liabilities/debts and tracking that number over time.

If you've been using a tracking app, you may already know your net worth. This is because most of these platforms will automatically calculate it for you based on the information you provide them—but you must provide the correct information. For an accurate net worth figure, you need to enter the value of all your assets and account for all your liabilities (amounts you owe).

You'll be calculating and recording your net worth in each Freak Phase, and it is best to do this precisely four months apart. Keeping a record of your net worth can be a source of insight and even inspiration as you watch it grow over time.

Here is an example of how to keep track of your net worth:

DATE	TOTAL ASSETS	TOTAL LIABILITES	NET WORTH

✢ Put a **RECURRING REMINDER** in your calendar to calculate and record your net worth every Phase.

Pay Yourself First at Least 30 Percent of Your Income

In Chapter Twenty-One of *First to a Million,* I introduce the key concept of "paying yourself first," which enables you to crush Mechanism 3, *save the difference.* If you pay yourself first at least 30 percent of your income and then invest that money wisely, you cannot help but reach FI early in life.

PAYING YOURSELF FIRST: Routinely and automatically putting money into savings and investments before spending on anything else.

Set up your monthly budget so that you automatically pay yourself first at least 30 percent of your income. The best way to do this is with an automatic monthly transfer of a certain amount from your checking account into your savings account. (Talk to your bank representative for help setting up this auto transfer.) Of course, you should do this only if you have regular income deposited into your checking account, because you can't transfer money that is not there to begin with.

 UTILIZING AUTOMATIC TRANSFERS: Employing a bank's customer platform features to program recurring transfers of money from one account to another.

If your income is irregular, you may need to manually transfer 30 percent of your income whenever you receive it. In that case, setting a recurring reminder in your calendar for every couple of weeks to review any income you've received and make sure your desired "pay yourself first percentage" gets transferred into your savings account can be helpful.

No matter what system you end up using, begin this life-changing habit *now*.

MY **"PAY YOURSELF FIRST"** PERCENT-AGE FOR EACH MONTH IN THIS PHASE WILL BE:

✚ Put a **RECURRING REMINDER** in your calendar to complete this task every month.

Calculate and Track Your Savings Rate

Friends and family may even complain that you're not really enjoying life. It helps to remember that you're not depriving yourself by spending less. Instead, you're consciously choosing to "spend" it on something much better than "stuff"—your freedom!

—CHAD CARSON, *RETIRE EARLY WITH REAL ESTATE*

Another finance-tracking tool is to calculate your savings rate every month. Go back and review Chapter Twenty-One in *First to a Million* to complete this task. In that chapter, I explain what a savings rate is, give detailed guidance on calculating your savings rate, and suggest a savings rate for all FI Freaks.

 TRACKING YOUR SAVINGS RATE: Regularly determining the percentage of money you save from your income and monitoring that number over time.

Your savings rate will often be different from your "pay yourself first" rate, because there will be months where you can save more than what you pay yourself first. Calculate your savings rate a few days after each month has ended. For example, do your calculation on the seventh of each month for the previous month. This allows enough time for all your transactions from the prior month to process and show up in your income and expenses tracking platform. Record your monthly savings rate in the same place as your net worth.

In *First to a Million,* I set the bar with a suggested savings rate of 50 percent or more. For a teenager living at home, this is an achievable goal. Once you move out, that can be a very high bar until you have a steady income.

If you choose to go to college, the 50 percent savings rate will be tough to hit, since your income will be low compared to the expenses involved with going to school. But if you choose to start full-time work after graduating from high school, the 50 percent benchmark will be much more achievable.

The bottom line is to be honest with yourself. Whatever situation you find yourself in, ask yourself this question: "Am I being diligent about saving money versus spending money?" If the answer is yes, then go easy on yourself. If your savings rate drops for a month or two, that's okay—some expenses can be pretty sporadic. Don't become a slave to your monthly savings rate.

A clearer picture of your success will emerge when you calculate your savings rate for the entire year. If you have kept an accurate record of your monthly numbers, you can easily calculate your yearly savings rate. Remember:

$$Savings\ Rate = Money\ Saved \div Money\ Earned.$$

Here is an example of how to track your savings rate:

DATE	SAVINGS RATE GOAL	MONEY EARNED	MONEY SAVED	SAVINGS RATE

✚ Put a **RECURRING REMINDER** in your calendar to complete this task every month.

MY **SAVINGS RATE GOAL** FOR EACH MONTH IN THIS PHASE IS:	

✚ Put a **RECURRING REMINDER** in your calendar on **JANUARY 15TH** to calculate your annual savings rate for the previous year.

Evaluate Your Core Circle

To successfully change my future, I had to change my thoughts and, as a result, the people I spent time with. Choose to spend time with people who understand and appreciate your vision and goals. Even better, choose people who share them!

—ROBERT KIYOSAKI, *RICH DAD POOR DAD FOR TEENS*

Just like your network, your "core circle" can change the course of your life for the better. Your core circle contains the four or five people you interact with the most. These are the people who have the greatest influence on how you spend your time each and every day.

FREAK SPEAK

FS **CORE CIRCLE:** The four or five people you spend the most time interacting with on a day-to-day basis.

Think about the people who are in your core circle today. What do you spend your time doing? What topics do you discuss most often? What activities do you do together?

Now answer these questions: Does the time I spend with my core circle advance me toward my goals? Do we talk about ideas? Do we do things that make me a better person or grow my worth as a human being? Do I regularly feel challenged because of my interactions with these people?

Your answers to some of these questions might be somewhat tough to acknowledge. I am not telling you to abandon your best friend tomorrow because they don't challenge you or help you meet your goals.

I am suggesting that you simply reconsider the amount of time you spend with the people in your core circle, as well as how they help you find success.

Simple minds discuss other people. Average minds discuss current events. And enlightened minds discuss ideas. If you are reading this, you know you are Freakish. Part of that identity is the fact that you love learning about different ideas and finding new challenges. You are Freakish, therefore you have an enlightened mind. To cultivate and develop your mind, you need to increase the number of conversations and experiences you have with like-minded people. New ideas and opportunities will begin to manifest when you do this. For example, I never considered writing a book until I started hanging out with people who had written books.

Here are some ways you can start increasing the time you spend with like-minded people:

- Connect with other Freaks on the SheeksFreaks platforms. The members are young, enlightened, and Freakish, just like you.
- Create a small group of similar people and regularly connect with them on Zoom meetings, group texts, or FaceTime calls.
- Start a club based on investing, finance, or real estate at your high school or college.
- Find and join a book club that focuses on mindset or personal growth.

Write down three goals regarding the time you spend with like-minded people and some action steps to reach them:

Start a Side Hustle

Time is your biggest asset. I reflected upon my habits and realized that I had wasted a lot of my own precious time. Hours were spent watching [sports] or mind-numbing TV, gossiping with friends, scrolling through social media—and quite frankly, this realization made me feel quite ashamed. Had I spent just 10 percent of that time on my own development and learning new skills, my career would have advanced sooner, and my income would have been a lot more comfortable for me.

—ATCHUTA NEELAM, "9 THINGS I WISH I HAD KNOWN WHEN I WAS 20," BIGGERPOCKETS BLOG

In Freak Phase 1, you had the task of getting a job. Hopefully, that is going well, and you are starting to build your income (Mechanism 1). But a Freak doesn't settle for one income source—it's time to start your first side hustle.

 SIDE HUSTLE: A job or money-making activity one can engage in outside of being a full-time student or employee.

If you think you don't have the time to start a new revenue stream, don't sweat it. Your first side hustle doesn't have to be something enormous, intricate, or abundantly profitable. It can be something simple, like baking and selling cookies at neighborhood events or walking your neighbor's dog when they work late. If you are ambitious, many types of side hustles offer more potential. The sky is the limit!

Remember, you only need to start *one* side hustle during this Phase to complete this task. The goal is to start thinking and behaving like an entrepreneur and a FI Freak when it comes to making more money. The lessons and experiences involved with any side hustle will become an essential foundation for your FI journey.

Most good side hustles take time to get off the ground. Therefore, you may not realize the side hustle's income potential or scalability right away. Also, make sure your side hustle is something you like—or even better, love—doing. If you don't, it probably won't last.

You'll likely experience one or two Freak Failures as you explore different side hustles. Creating a successful and sustainable side hustle is not easy. If it were, everyone would do it. You may put hours and hours (and perhaps dollars and dollars) into building a side hustle, only to see it fail.

FREAK FAILURE: A failure that seems like a loss but is actually a win in that it brings experience, knowledge, and connections that will help you succeed in the future.

Your first side hustle probably won't be a major success or earn you lots of income. You may have to try two—or three or four—and fail before you find one that works for you. We don't know how many you'll have to fail at until you find the one that generates incredible income. But we do know you won't get to that successful side hustle until you start your first one.

Review Chapter Sixteen in *First to a Million* for many side hustle ideas. For even more possibilities, visit biggerpockets.com/teenworkbook. After reviewing these ideas, make a list of side hustles you might like to start. Then narrow it down to one, and get started!

POSSIBLE SIDE HUSTLES

Congratulations! You've just completed Freak Phase 2! It's time to be proud of your Freakishness and check in with your progress. Post a video of yourself describing the three most meaningful tasks you completed in this Freak Phase, and post a picture of yourself with your completed checklist from the beginning of this Phase.

Don't forget to use **#FREAKPHASE2** and **#TEENAGEFIFREAK** and to tag **@SHEEKSFREAKS** and **@BIGGERPOCKETS!**

Now
GO OUT THERE
and Get Your
FREAK ON!

FREAK PHASE *Three*

JANUARY–APRIL
Second semester of junior year of high school

The thing I would say to the person who wants success, who wants wealth, who wants money, who wants growth, is to realize that you will want those things no matter what stage of life you are in. It's the pursuit that you want… If you can realize that the [fulfillment] comes when you stop putting the result on a pedestal and you just start [enjoying] the excitement you think is going to be on the other end of the result, then you're freed up. And you get to experience all of the [fulfillment] now. Not when you have the million-dollar business. Not when you've got a certain amount of money in the bank. But right now.

—RYAN DANIEL MORAN, "JUST START," *CAPITALISM.COM WITH RYAN DANIEL MORAN* PODCAST

Here is the checklist for this four-month Freak Phase. It's best to read the entire Freak Phase before filling in the due date for each item. Don't forget to use your calendar to help you stay on track. And remember—you're a FI Freak, so you've got this!

DUE DATES	✓	TASK
	○	Read *The Richest Man in Babylon* by George Clason.
	○	Continue networking.
	○	Evaluate your income streams.
	○	Evaluate your transportation costs.
	○	Speak to a school counselor about next year's classes.
	○	Review your happiness list.
	○	Learn more about real estate investing.
	○	Set three financial goals.
	○	Implement a new Freak Tweak.
	○	Sell a personal item you no longer need or want.
	○	Find and do a new fun, free activity.
	○	Interview someone who is where you want to be.
	○	Calculate and track your net worth.

Goals
+ACTION STEPS

DATE: _____

The date I communicated my three goals to my accountability partner.

Write out your three goals for this Freak Phase here.

1 ....

2 ....

3 ....

MY NEW "PAY YOURSELF FIRST"
PERCENTAGE
GOAL IS:
%

MY NEW
SAVINGS RATE
GOAL IS:
%

MONTH 1 / DATE COMPLETED

....

PERSON TO INTERVIEW

....

MONTH 2 / DATE COMPLETED

....

PERSON TO INTERVIEW

....

MONTH 3 / DATE COMPLETED

....

PERSON TO INTERVIEW

....

MONTH 4 / DATE COMPLETED

....

PERSON TO INTERVIEW

....

FOR FRUGALITY IS...

✢ Put a **RECURRING REMINDER** in your calendar to complete these tasks at the
✢ beginning of every Freak Phase.

Understand that accumulating a lifetime of wealth in a short period of time involves making personal decisions in major areas of your life that are different than the norm. It involves working harder and smarter than the average [student or] employee, and it involves making different career decisions than the Average Joe . . . In short, it involves a change of perspective that may be sharply at odds from that of your family, friends, and [peers].

—SCOTT TRENCH, *SET FOR LIFE*

Read *The Richest Man in Babylon*

This book written by George Clason is considered a must-read by many in the FIRE and REI communities. It contains a series of straightforward lessons that teach you how to think about and use money.

Continue Networking

I cannot overstate the importance and value of networking to connect with like-minded FI Freaks! This can change everything for you in the blink of an eye. You simply have no idea what opportunity or new idea will come from your networking efforts that can completely change your life. You *need* to be networking!

In the last Phase, you started your networking efforts. You created accounts on LinkedIn, BiggerPockets, and SheeksFreaks. This is a great way to find people to build your network. But simply following or connecting with them on the platform is not enough. You need to actually have conversations with people.

Interviewing someone is one way to form a more meaningful connection, but you can also connect through phone calls, side conversations at meetups, Zoom meetings, or FaceTime chats. You could reach out through emails, DMs on Instagram, or messages sent through LinkedIn, BiggerPockets, and SheeksFreaks. Or you might post your questions or goals on any online platform to see who responds. Choose a few methods that are a good fit for you and hammer them!

To maximize your networking efforts over time, you need to start a list of the people you interact with. (I recommend a Google Sheet.) On that list, include:
- Their name
- Their contact info (phone number, email address, or account profile)
- What they do
- Where they live (including their time zone)
- What you've talked about
- Where you met them
- The last time you interacted with them
- Any other relevant information

Go back to Freak Phase 2 for reminders on how to maximize your networking efforts.

✦➕ Put a **RECURRING REMINDER** in your calendar to complete this task every Phase.

List some actions, events, or strategies you'll complete during each month of this Phase to build your network. Put any needed reminders in your calendar.

MONTH 1

MONTH 2

MONTH 3

Evaluate Your Income Streams

It's beneficial to evaluate your income streams every Phase to see if you should make any changes to your revenue-generating efforts as you hammer Mechanism 1. When evaluating them, take a step back and analyze your efforts from a high-level view.

FREAK TECHNIQUE

EVALUATING INCOME STREAMS: Periodically reviewing all your income streams to see if you're using your time and energy for maximum results.

In Phase 1, one of your tasks was to get a job. This occurred in the summer, when most high school students have plenty of time to work and earn some money. Hopefully, you've been able to continue working on a part-time basis during this school year.

In Phase 2, one of the tasks was to begin a side hustle. At this point, you've been doing that for a few months. There are many side hustles to choose from, so reviewing an active side hustle's success is essential to see if it should be continued or replaced. Since time is our most valuable resource, we want to make sure we're using it to the best of our ability.

If you are working a part-time job, write out the answers to these questions:

Q. Is this job providing me all the hours I want?

A.

Q. Is this job providing me with a safe and enjoyable work environment?

A.

Q. Is this job paying me a fair wage?

A.

Q. Can I see myself working this job for another year or two?

A.

Q. Are there other part-time jobs available that would pay more?

A.

Q. Do I have friends or family who can help me find a better-paying, safer, or more enjoyable job?

A.

Based on your answers to these questions, spend some time considering your options. Also, go over these questions and answers with a parent to get their perspective.

If you are not working a part-time job, ask yourself these questions:

Q. Why am I not working a part-time job right now?

A.

Q. If the answer was "time," is that an excuse or a reality? Do I have a few hours of free time on the weekends that I could spend earning some money at a job?

A.

Q. When could I start working a part-time job? What can I do now to increase my chances of finding a desirable job when the time comes?

A.

A side hustle is different from a part-time job when it comes to evaluating income. Some side hustles take time to develop. You may have spent the past few months getting your side hustle started and are just now starting to see some results (income). Or maybe those results are yet to come. Being patient with a side hustle can pay off significantly in the future.

Ask yourself these questions about your side hustle:

Q. If I have yet to earn any income from the side hustle, how much longer until that happens? Am I working hard to make that day come sooner rather than later?

A.

Q. How much potential does my side hustle have? Is it scalable? Can I see it growing in the future?

A.

Q. Do I enjoy the time I put into my side hustle? If not, what other options might I consider that would be more enjoyable? (See your list from the end of Phase 2.)

A.

Q. What else needs to happen for my side hustle to grow and prosper? What resources could I use? Who might I talk to for advice?

A.

Q. Am I keeping track of my income from my side hustle when I track my income and expenses? (Knowing your total revenue is helpful when periodically evaluating a side hustle.)

A.

Based on the answers to these questions about part-time jobs and side hustles, what action steps should I take during this Phase to improve my income-generating efforts? **Put any necessary reminders (one-time or recurring) in your calendar.**

ACTION STEPS
FOR THIS FREAK PHASE

1.

2.

3.

4.

5.

Evaluate Your Transportation Costs

As a high school student, you may or may not have a car. If you do, then this task is crucial for you. If you don't, it's still important because at some point you will consider buying a car. Saving money (Mechanism 2) is critical, and transportation costs are among the top three expenses that can hamper your efforts to spend less. Go back and review the "Transportation Expenses" section of Chapter Eighteen in *First to a Million* to refresh your memory of the hidden (and considerable) costs of owning a car.

Once you've reviewed Chapter Eighteen and read the three blog posts linked at biggerpockets.com/teenworkbook, you should evaluate your transportation costs. If you own a car, what does it cost you? Fill out the chart below to find out. When you're done, ask yourself if the yearly expense of owning a car is really worth it to you. If your parents are paying for most or all of your car's expenses, what's the plan after you graduate? Will they continue to pay for those expenses?

If you have a car, list the related expenses below to see how much it's costing you per year:

EXPENSE	AMOUNT	x 12 MONTHS	TOTAL PER YEAR
Gas (monthly)		x 12	
Car loan payment (monthly)		x 12	
Insurance (monthly)		x 12	
Parking (monthly)		x 12	
Regular maintenance (annual—e.g., oil changes, tire rotations)		– – – – – – – – →	
Registration (annual)		– – – – – – – – →	
Depreciation (annual)		– – – – – – – – →	
Repairs (annual)		– – – – – – – – →	

TOTALY YEARLY EXPENSE $

If this number is not acceptable to you, it's time to reconsider your transportation and find a solution. Selling your car can be a courageous step toward early FI. Riding a bike, using an electric scooter/bike, or taking public transportation are all options that may be better for your Freakish future. Selling your car to purchase a more affordable one can also be a wise move—especially if you have a car loan!

✚ Put a **RECURRING REMINDER** in your calendar to use this chart and evaluate your transportation costs once a year.

If you have a car (or will get one soon), put a recurring reminder in your calendar to take your car in for regular maintenance (oil changes, tire rotations, complete inspection) once a year. This proactive habit will save you lots of money on unexpected repairs down the road.

Speak to a School Counselor About Next Year's Classes

At some point during this Phase, you'll be registering for classes for your senior year. Set aside some time to choose your classes carefully, and take advantage of valuable classes while they are free. At the beginning of Chapter Twenty-Seven in *First to a Million*, I list some high school classes you should consider and other class options to utilize while in high school. Review this information now.

Then, make an appointment with your school counselor to talk about your classes for next year. Explain your goals and ambitions and why you think certain classes will help build your future. Listen to their advice, but also do what you think is best for you.

Put any needed reminders in your calendar that will help you accomplish this task.

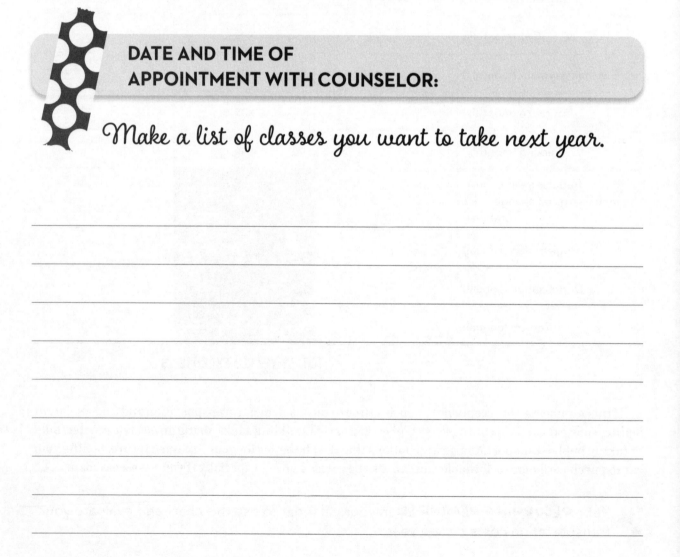

DATE AND TIME OF APPOINTMENT WITH COUNSELOR:

Make a list of classes you want to take next year.

_____

_____

_____

_____

_____

_____

_____

Review Your Happiness List

Action may not always bring happiness, but there is no happiness without action.

—ATTRIBUTED TO BENJAMIN DISRAELI

The goal is happiness—each and every day—so let's review and update your happiness list. You copied your happiness list from *First to a Million* into the introduction of this workbook. Look it over and then answer the questions below.

 REVIEWING YOUR HAPPINESS LIST: Doing a regular inventory of activities that bring happiness and joy into your life.

Q. Have I been engaging in these activities regularly?
A.

Q. Which ones have I forgotten that I should do more often?
A.

Q. Are there any new additions? Subtractions? (You don't need to have precisely ten items on the list.)
A.

Q. Am I sacrificing happiness during my journey to early FI? If so, how do I stop that now?
A.

✦ Put a **RECURRING REMINDER** in your calendar to review and update your happiness list once a year.

Learn More About Real Estate Investing

Give me six hours to chop down a tree, and I will spend the first four sharpening my axe.

—UNKNOWN

I'm sure you remember from *First to a Million* that real estate investing (REI) is one of the two main ways to invest your money (Mechanism 4). But learning how to invest in real estate may seem daunting and intimidating.

If REI seems too scary for you now, have some patience. The key to success—just as for a logger chopping down a tree—is lots of careful preparation.

At this age, you have a few years to prepare yourself for REI before buying your first property. By learning as much as you can now, you'll go from feeling intimidated and confused to a place of confidence and readiness. When the time comes, you'll bring down that tree with ease!

As you check off tasks in the *First to a Million* workbook, you'll be exposed to many REI pathways and strategies by listening to podcasts; reading books, articles, and blog posts; and talking to other people.

If you do choose to invest a good portion of your savings in real estate to earn passive income for the rest of your life, get ready to hear some of these standard warnings from cynics:

- What if real estate values plummet?
- What if the rental market goes flat?
- What if you have a nightmare tenant and they don't pay rent for several months?
- Have you thought about all the things you'll need to take care of?
- Are you sure you want to be responsible for someone else's living situation?
- Couldn't someone sue you if they were injured on your property?
- Wouldn't you feel safer if your money was in the stock market?

First, let me assure you that we will be addressing all these issues throughout this workbook and in the resources it points you to. There are legitimate ways to deal with each of these situations. But second, remember that *every* investment involves risk, and there are ways to minimize the risks that come with REI.

Got to biggerpockets.com/teenworkbook for the link to a twenty-page PDF titled *Seven Years to Seven Figure Wealth* by Brandon Turner. It focuses on building wealth through REI and is an excellent introduction to the impact REI can have on your future. Since we will be diving much deeper into REI in upcoming Phases, this introductory read will lay the foundation for what is to come.

Write your five main takeaways from *Seven Years to Seven Figure Wealth* on the next page:

Congratulations! You've just completed Freak Phase 3! It's time to be proud of your Freakishness and check in with your progress. Post a video of yourself describing the three most meaningful tasks you completed in this Freak Phase, and post a picture of yourself with your completed checklist from the beginning of this Phase.

Don't forget to use **#FREAKPHASE3** and **#TEENAGEFiFREAK** and to tag **@SHEEKSFREAKS** and **@BIGGERPOCKETS!**

NOW GO OUT THERE AND GET YOUR

FREAK ON!

FREAK PHASE *Four*

MAY–AUGUST

Summer between junior and senior year of high school

People who are rich are usually good at generating passive income. Their money is working for them while they're working in other ways— managing their portfolio, starting other businesses, or simply enjoying their lives.

ROBERT KIYOSAKI, *RICH DAD POOR DAD FOR TEENS*

Here is the checklist for this four-month Freak Phase. It's best to read the entire Freak Phase before filling in the due date for each item. Don't forget to use your calendar to help you stay on track. And remember—you're a FI Freak, so you've got this!

DUE DATES	✓	TASK
	○	Read *The Millionaire Next Door* by Thomas J. Stanley and William D. Danko.
	○	Evaluate your income streams.
	○	Shadow someone for a day.
	○	Find a mentor.
	○	Start a passive income stream.
	○	Start creating content.
	○	Review your Why of FI list.
	○	Continue to learn about real estate investing.
	○	Set three financial goals.
	○	Implement a new Freak Tweak.
	○	Sell a personal item you no longer need or want.
	○	Find and do a new fun, free activity.
	○	Interview someone who is where you want to be.
	○	Calculate and track your net worth.
	○	Continue networking.

DATE: _____

The date I communicated my three goals to my accountability partner.

Write out your three goals for this Freak Phase here.

1 ....

2 ....

3 ....

MY NEW "PAY YOURSELF FIRST"
PERCENTAGE GOAL IS:
%

MY NEW
SAVINGS RATE GOAL IS:
%

INTERVIEW Log

MONTH 1 / DATE COMPLETED

....

PERSON TO INTERVIEW

....

MONTH 2 / DATE COMPLETED

....

PERSON TO INTERVIEW

....

MONTH 3 / DATE COMPLETED

....

PERSON TO INTERVIEW

....

MONTH 4 / DATE COMPLETED

....

PERSON TO INTERVIEW

....

My New FREAK Tweak

FOR FRUGALITY IS...

Put a **RECURRING REMINDER** in your calendar to complete these tasks at the beginning of every Freak Phase.

Read *The Millionaire Next Door*

This famous book details surprising research findings about the "American millionaire." Contrary to popular belief, the average millionaire does not have a mansion with several fancy luxury cars. Instead, they have a modest home, drive a used car, and save money like a FI Freak. Most of their friends and neighbors have no idea they are millionaires because they choose to *be* wealthy instead of *look* wealthy.

Evaluate Your Income Streams

It looks like nothing's happening. Most people give up when nothing's happening. [But] eventually . . . you hit this exponential curve.

—RYAN DANIEL MORAN, "1,000 DAY GOALS," *CAPITALISM.COM WITH RYAN DANIEL MORAN* PODCAST

When starting a side hustle, many people see little reward for all their effort. They may have put hours of work and perhaps hundreds (or even thousands) of dollars into building the side hustle, only to achieve minimal results. With that in mind, let's take a quick look at the Hockey Stick Principle.

The Hockey Stick Principle

To have success, one generally must put in a lot of work before they start to see results. Only after significant time and effort will rewards start to show up. If you were to chart the success of most meaningful endeavors, it generally looks like a hockey stick—long and horizontal, with a sudden upward slope. The success is flat over a period of time (month or years), and then finally, the time, energy, and money invested start to take off.

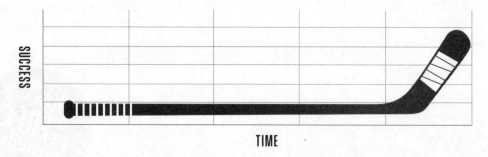

When looking at successful entrepreneurs, we tend to see the last part of their journey—the exponential growth part. Since that's all we see, they can appear to be overnight successes. For example, we may hear of a person who has a business that starts to blow up (in a good way). Or we may read about someone who launched a new product and is making millions. Or we might know someone who was in the right place at the right time and is now making tons of money by filling a need in the marketplace. (Think of Jeff Bezos, Bill Gates, and Elon Musk.)

What we don't see is all the effort these people put in before achieving their success. Years of research, study, work, and failures put them in a position to succeed when that hockey stick of success finally started to climb.

It's very similar to your early FI pathway. You'll be putting in a ton of work during the first few years of your journey while you learn, read, study, analyze, save, and fail. Although your successes will be minor at first, your efforts will eventually pay off when the success level begins to rapidly climb at the end of your hockey stick. These successes will manifest as cash flow, tax benefits, compounding interest, mortgage paydowns, rising net worth, property appreciation, unforeseen opportunities, and more.

So if your side hustle hasn't taken off, you might not want to give up just yet: Exponential success could be right around the corner! Of course, it is possible that your side hustle will never take off. Whether to quit or stay the course can be a tough choice, but if you believe in your heart that your current side hustle has potential, I urge you to keep working your way across the hockey stick.

Evaluation for This Phase

In the last Phase, you evaluated your income streams for the first time. It's beneficial to do this every Phase to see if you should make any changes to your revenue-generating efforts as you hammer Mechanism 1. When you evaluate them, take a step back and analyze your efforts from a high-level view. When life is busy—and it usually is—we can get caught up in the day-to-day grind. In that state, it's almost impossible to look at things from a long-term strategic viewpoint. Take some time now to do just that.

How are your part-time job and side hustle going? If necessary, go back to Phase 3 for some questions you can ask yourself when evaluating these two income streams.

Based on the answers to those questions, what

ACTION STEPS FOR THIS
FREAK PHASE TO INCREASE INCOME

1.

2.

3.

4.

5.

✚ Put a RECURRING REMINDER in your calendar to complete this task every Phase.

action steps should you take during this Phase to improve your income-generating efforts? Put any necessary reminders (one-time or recurring) in your calendar.

Shadow Someone for a Day

Now that you have begun to make some quality contacts through your networking efforts, you're ready to take the next step. Set up a day and time to shadow someone who works in a career, industry, or profession that is interesting to you. Contact them and ask if you can shadow them for a day. It may be best to wait until you are out of school for the summer, so you'll have more flexibility.

On the day of your shadow, dress well and be on time. Print out some questions you would like to ask and take them with you. These could be about the person's mindset, their projects, and their current struggles in business. Be honest about what you know and don't know.

Once the day is over, send the person you shadowed a thank-you card or email. Keep in touch, and add them to your networking list if they are not already there.

Questions I Will Ask

1.

2.

3.

4.

5.

6.

7.

8.

9.

10.

✦ Put a **RECURRING REMINDER** in your calendar to complete this task every Phase.

Find a Mentor

I'm going to tell you a secret: Old people like ambitious young people . . . There is something truly rewarding about helping an ambitious young person achieve their goals. I think a lot of it has to do with "I see myself in their shoes" or "If only I had started back then!"

—BRANDON TURNER, "HOW TO START INVESTING IN REAL ESTATE AT A YOUNG AGE," BIGGERPOCKETS BLOG

Finding a quality mentor will be a massive boost to both your knowledge and your motivation. You will be able to bounce ideas off your mentor, and they will give you advice on how to avoid making the same mistakes they did. Most successful people will be more than eager to help someone as young and motivated as you. They will appreciate the energy, hustle, and passion you bring to the table.

FREAK SPEAK

MENTOR: An experienced and trusted advisor who shares information about their career path, serves as a role model, and provides guidance, motivation, and emotional support. A mentor may also help you with evaluating careers, creating contacts, and setting goals.

Choosing the right mentor is not easy. And once you've identified someone, it can be even more challenging to actually get them to *be* your mentor. (Of course, the more people you interview and shadow, the more likely you are to find a mentor!)

Once you have an excellent idea of the job or career you would like to pursue, you're ready to begin. Think of everyone you know. Ask around. Evaluate the connections you've made building your network. A fitting mentor is likely somewhere in that network. Once you've decided on a specific person, ask them to meet you for coffee or lunch. It's *always* best to meet in person than to have a phone call, Zoom meeting, or email correspondence.

Do *not* ask someone to be your mentor the first time you meet them. The most productive relationships start slowly and organically. You are more likely to find a mentor in someone you have already interviewed, shadowed, or connected with than someone you have just asked out of the blue.

When you first connect with a potential mentor, be cautious about bombarding them with questions. You don't want to scare people away. Ask a few meaningful yet straightforward questions that encourage your mentor to do most of the talking. (Most people like to talk about themselves.) Here are some strategic questions you might ask. (These are also great questions for an interview or a shadow day!) Don't forget to take a notebook and write stuff down.

- How did you get into this job or career?
- What's the one thing that made the most significant difference in your journey?
- If you were doing it again, what would you do differently?
- If you weren't doing this, what would you be doing?
- How can I help you with one of your current projects?

A great way to begin the relationship is to add value to their work. This could be as simple as helping with some office tasks or cleaning up debris on a house they are fixing up. Always be respectful of their time (don't be late), and genuinely thank them for meeting with you. At the end of your meeting, or in a follow-up thank-you email, ask if you can shadow them or help them at their place of work. Pretty soon, you may have a mentor/mentee relationship without ever mentioning the word "mentor." It will have happened organically over a period of time.

Your first try at securing a mentor could result in a Freak Failure. In fact, you may fail a few times, but each try will bring you success in other ways. Don't give up!

Refer to biggerpockets.com/teenworkbook for a blog post with more guidance for finding a mentor.

If you are unsure about who your mentor should be, it is okay to postpone this task. Just put a reminder in your calendar to come back to this in a few months or a year.

NAME	PROFESSION/ WORKPLACE	CONTACT INFO

✚ Put a **RECURRING REMINDER** in your calendar to touch base with your mentor at least twice a month.

Start a Passive Income Stream

In Chapter Fourteen of *First to a Million*, we went over the life-changing concept of passive income. You should review that chapter if needed. It's now time to add another income stream to your portfolio—a passive income stream—in order to continue dominating Mechanism 1.

 PASSIVE INCOME: Income you receive when not actively working.

There are many types of passive income. Some require a major time investment up front, while others don't. Some require a lot of money up front, while others don't. And some produce more passive income than others. The passive income stream you choose to pursue will depend on your specific interests and situation.

Look over this list to start getting ideas of passive income streams that may work for you. This is *not* an all-inclusive list. You can google more options if needed.

- Buying rental properties
- Owning vending machines
- Owning self-serve car washes
- Owning laundromats
- Owning self-storage rentals
- Selling an e-book you've written
- Selling stock photos you've taken
- Selling an online course you've created
- Investing in dividend stocks
- Investing in real estate investment trusts (REITs)
- Putting money in high-yield savings accounts
- Renting out your garage
- Getting paid to put an ad on your car
- Renting out your car on Turo

Refer to biggerpockets.com/teenworkbook for two blog posts with more information about passive income.

Your task is to begin one passive income stream, so start with a few options and then narrow them down. To begin, write down some of your top choices and what your next step is below.

PASSIVE INCOME OPTION

_____

_____

_____

_____

NEXT STEP TO BEGIN

_____

_____

_____

_____

Start Creating Content

While navigating your journey to early FI, you should choose a creative way to document your experiences, both good and bad.

FREAK TECHNIQUE

CREATING CONTENT: Documenting your journey by using your creativity to develop original content that broadens your network and gains you support.

There are several platforms to choose from, and you're probably more familiar with them than I am. Choose one you know well (or take a risk with one you don't), set up a new account, and start creating. Here are just a few ideas of where you can document your journey and get creative:

- Start a podcast
- Start a blog
- Start a YouTube channel
- Start a website
- Use your TikTok, Instagram, or Facebook account

Create content for your platform regularly, but don't let it distract you from your other obligations. Posting a couple of times a week should be enough—just be sure to do so regularly. After a year, you'll be amazed at how much content you have, how much the quality has increased, and how interesting it is for you to look back at earlier content.

Make a list of your top three choices for creating content. Then list the next step to begin each. In the end, choose one.

CREATIVE PLATFORM	NEXT STEP TO BEGIN

✦ Put a **RECURRING REMINDER** in your calendar to post or publish at least twice a week.

Review Your Why of FI List

Your motivation to pursue early FI is embedded in your Why of FI list, which you copied from *First to a Million* into this workbook's introduction. Go back and look it over while answering the following questions:

 REVIEWING YOUR WHY OF FI LIST: Digging deep within yourself to identify your foundational reasons for becoming a FI Freak.

Q. Have my lower-level whys changed?
A.

Q. Are my higher-level whys still accurate?
A.

Q. When I reach early FI, how would I most prefer to be of service to others?
A.

Q. What provides my daily dose of drive and motivation?
A.

Q. Has someone else's Why of FI resonated with me?
A.

⁺⁺ Put a **RECURRING REMINDER** in your calendar to review and update your Why of FI list once a year.

Continue to Learn About Real Estate Investing

There's a lot to know about real estate investing. The very idea of it can be very intimidating to rookies. But following the steps laid out in the *First to a Million* workbook will help you be well prepared in time to buy your first property. Let's take this opportunity to learn some more.

Common Reasons To Avoid REI

Some of you may be accustomed to getting straight As in school or scoring 100 percent on your tests. If so, you are used to knowing everything you need to know. You *cannot* have this mindset in REI! You'll never know *everything*, and you don't need to. You only need to know enough to get started. You'll learn everything else as you need to know it.

As you start to invest in real estate, your immediate need to know something will force you to research and learn at the appropriate time. For example, let's say the first property you buy happens to be a duplex and you don't know how to separate utilities for the two units. You'll learn fast by researching on Google and YouTube, as well as within various forums. So don't get stalled now by focusing on what you don't know.

In addition to thinking they need to know everything from the start, many people have other reasons for not wanting to be a landlord or a property owner. They tell themselves that:

- Tenants will screw me over.
- Things are going to break.
- Tenants are going to call me in the middle of the night.
- Someone is going to trip on my property and sue me.

Those are just excuses. If they were legitimate reasons to not invest in real estate, no one would do it. Yet many *very* successful people do. Instead of coming up with excuses, find solutions:

Excuse: Tenants will screw me over.
Solution: Have near-bulletproof screening procedures and ironclad leases.

Excuse: Things are going to break.
Solution: Hire a handyperson.

Excuse: Tenants will call me in the middle of the night.
Solution: Hire an answering service—or better yet, a property manager.

Excuse: Someone is going to trip on my property and sue me.
Solution: Buy insurance.

It's time to level up your engagement on the BiggerPockets website to learn more about REI and quash some of your fears. Complete the following chart by entering the goals you wish to reach by the end of this Phase.

ACTIVITY	# OF TIMES I'LL DO IT THIS PHASE
1. Post in the forums	
2. Comment on someone else's forum post	
3. Read a blog post	
4. Tune in to a live webinar	
5. Watch a BiggerPockets YouTube video	
6. Message another member	

Congratulations! You've just completed Freak Phase 4! It's time to be proud of your Freakishness and check in with your progress. Post a video of yourself describing the three most meaningful tasks you completed in this Freak Phase, and post a picture of yourself with your completed checklist from the beginning of this Phase.

Don't forget to use **#FREAKPHASE4** and **#TEENAGEFIFREAK** and to tag **@SHEEKSFREAKS** and **@BIGGERPOCKETS!**

NOW GO OUT THERE AND GET YOUR *Freak On!*

FREAK PHASE Four 1/2

THE DAY YOU TURN 18
(postpone this until your birthday)

Once you have reached financial independence, you are no longer tied down to your salaried job. You don't have to quit, but you have the option to. After achieving financial independence, you can confidently walk into your boss's office and ask for a raise, extended time off, to work remotely, or anything else that will make your day-to-day life more enjoyable.

—CRAIG CURELOP, "IF YOU'RE PURSUING FINANCIAL INDEPENDENCE, YOU'LL FEEL DIFFERENT THAN EVERYONE—AND THAT'S OK," BIGGERPOCKETS BLOG

This Freak Phase is to be completed when you turn 18.

✦✚
✚✚ Put a **REMINDER** in your calendar to come back to this Phase on your 18TH BIRTHDAY.

Here is the checklist for this Freak Phase. It's best to read the entire Freak Phase before filling in the due date for each item. Don't forget to use your calendar to help you stay on track. And remember—you're a FI Freak, so you've got this!

DUE DATES	✓	TASK
	○	Get your first credit card.
	○	Open a checking account.
	○	Open three savings accounts.
	○	Choose your investing ratio.
	○	Open a brokerage account.

Goals
+ ACTION STEPS

DATE: _____

The date I communicated my three goals to my accountability partner.

Write out your three goals for this Freak Phase here.

1 ....

2 ....

3 ....

MY NEW "PAY YOURSELF FIRST"
PERCENTAGE
GOAL IS: %

MY NEW
SAVINGS RATE
GOAL IS: %

INTERVIEW Log

MONTH 1 / DATE COMPLETED

....

PERSON TO INTERVIEW

....

MONTH 2 / DATE COMPLETED

....

PERSON TO INTERVIEW

....

MONTH 3 / DATE COMPLETED

....

PERSON TO INTERVIEW

....

MONTH 4 / DATE COMPLETED

....

PERSON TO INTERVIEW

....

My New FREAK Tweak

FOR FRUGALITY IS...

✚ Put a **RECURRING REMINDER** in your calendar to complete these tasks at the beginning of every Freak Phase.

Get Your First Credit Card

Happy 18th birthday! Now that you've hit the magic number, you are legally considered an adult. That means you can vote, join the military, buy a lottery ticket, get a tattoo, and sign contracts. Oh, and you can open your own financial accounts!

Currently, you may be an authorized user on your parent's credit card. If so, you've already been building your credit score and credit history. I recommend you keep using that card (with your parent's permission, of course) until you turn 19 *and* apply now for your own credit card. If you are not an authorized user on a parent's credit card, then today is the day you start building your credit score and history.

In Chapter Eleven of *First to a Million,* we went over credit scores, and in Chapter Twelve we discussed credit cards. I highly recommend you review those chapters now. And for more information about choosing and managing your credit card, check out the blog posts at biggerpockets.com/teenworkbook.

Once you've reviewed all that information, apply for your own credit card. (Ideally, that would happen today.) Your first one will probably be a secured credit card, meaning you will have to pay a deposit. You should also inquire about a student credit card. You may choose to get your card from the bank where you already do business or from one of the big credit card companies. (These options are all covered in the blog posts.) When you receive the credit card, download that company's app so you can easily check your account whenever needed.

The key is to use your credit card only to buy things you would buy anyway, and to use it at least once a month. When you make your monthly payment on time (for the entire balance), you build your credit score. If you have a credit card and never use it, your credit score will not grow. So apply for that first card today and start your journey to an 800+ credit score!

To build your credit score even faster, I recommend getting a second card when you turn 19 and a third when you turn 19½. You should wait a year before getting your second card to prove to yourself you can handle the responsibility of one card. When you get your second and third cards, you'll need to use them as well. Plan on using one for food, one for gas or a monthly bill, and the third for everything else. By making three credit card payments on time every month, your will grow your credit score *quickly.*

Another strategy for increasing your credit score is to ask the credit card company to raise your credit limit. You should do this once a year. If they agree to raise your credit limit, your utilization rate (your average balance compared to the credit limit for the account) will go down, helping to raise your score.

✔ TO DO:

- Choose which credit card you want to apply for.

- Apply and get accepted for that credit card.

- Ask your parent if you can continue to use the card on which you're an authorized user (if applicable).

- Receive your new credit card in the mail.

- Make your first purchase on your new credit card.

- Make your first on-time payment of the full balance.

✳✚ Put a **REMINDER** in your calendar to apply for your second credit card on your **19TH** birthday. Once you've received that second credit card, have your parent remove you as an authorized user on their credit card (if applicable).

✳✚ Put a **REMINDER** in your calendar to apply for your third credit card when you turn **19½**. Put a recurring reminder in your calendar to call each credit card company once a year to ask about increasing your credit limit.

Open a Checking Account

You may have opened a checking account with a parent before turning 18. If so, you may now call the bank and inquire about taking your parent off your account. If you do not have a checking account, get one ASAP.

Ask whatever bank you choose if they have special accounts for teens. Sometimes the fees or requirements for these accounts will be lower, and they will be easier to open. Large national banks such as Bank of America, Chase, U.S. Bank, and Wells Fargo all have teen accounts.

If you are about to open your first checking account, refer back to the "Manage your checking and savings accounts like a Freak" task in Freak Phase 2. You should also read the blog posts at biggerpockets.com/teenworkbook.

Once your checking account is up and running, make sure to download the bank's app so you can easily monitor your account.

Use this list to create your plan to open your checking account. ➡

✓ **TO DO:**

○ Choose a bank.

○ Call the bank to set up an appointment.

○ Get ready for your appointment.

○ Open your checking account with the help of a bank representative.

○ Download the bank's app.

○ Receive your debit card in the mail.

Open Three Savings Accounts

In Chapter Twenty of *First to a Million,* we went over the importance of a savings account, how to open one, and how many you should have. Review that chapter, which focuses on Mechanism 3. If you are about to open your first savings account, also refer back to the "Manage your checking and savings accounts like a Freak" task in Freak Phase 2. For more important information about opening savings accounts, refer to the blog post at biggerpockets.com/teenworkbook.

You may have opened a savings account with a parent before turning 18. If so, you may now call the bank and inquire about taking your parent off your account. If you do not have a savings account, that is about to change.

Where To Open Your Savings Accounts

I recommend having your emergency fund savings account at a local bank. If you opened a savings account with your parent before turning 18 and it is at a local bank, use that one. If not, it will be convenient to open your emergency fund savings account at the same bank as your checking account.

The other two accounts—your future investment fund and your "fun" fund—can be at the same bank or an online bank. Having all your savings accounts at one bank can be very convenient. For example, moving money from one account to another is instantaneous if the accounts are at the same bank, but that transfer can take a few days if the accounts are at different banks. If you choose to open a checking account and a savings account at the same bank, you can open your other two savings accounts at the same time.

However, online banks offer higher interest rates than traditional banks. Therefore, opening your other two accounts with an online bank can earn you more free money (although it won't amount to much, because interest rates are at all-time lows as I write this workbook).

Ask whatever bank you choose if they have special accounts for teens. Sometimes the fees or requirements for teen accounts will be lower, and they will be easier to open. Large national banks such as Bank of America, Chase, U.S. Bank, and Wells Fargo all have teen accounts. The steps to open a savings account are very similar to those for opening a checking account. Make sure to download the apps for whichever banks you decide to use.

Savings Account No. 1: Emergency Fund

If you already have a savings account, it will now become your emergency fund account. You should keep enough money to cover six months' worth of expenses in this account. Since you have been tracking your income and expenses, you should be able to determine your average monthly expenses. Take that amount and multiply it by six. That is how much you should have in this account.

If you already have that much saved, good for you! If not, your first priority is to fully fund this account as soon as you can. Until you've done that, you will not be investing.

Savings Account No. 2: Future Investment Fund

You also need to open a savings account for future investments. If you have extra money to move out of your emergency fund account, it should go here. This will be the holding account for all money you plan to invest.

Savings Account No. 3: "Fun" Fund

As I explain in Chapter Twenty of *First to a Million,* this account is optional but highly recommended. It allows you to spend on larger or more expensive purchases. These would be "nonessential" items that you have not budgeted for in your checking account, such as a vacation, a new snowboard, or a new video game system. You deserve to buy these types of things from time to time if you save the money *before* you buy them.

When you do use this money, spend it wisely. Make the purchase with your credit card, and then pay off the entire credit card balance by using the money saved in this account. (You'll have to transfer the money from this account into your checking account first.) This way, you are taking full advantage of any rewards program your credit card may have.

Use this space to track your progress for opening your savings accounts.

ACCOUNT NAME	WHAT BANK WILL I USE?	DATE OPENED
EMERGENCY FUND		
EMERGENCY FUND		
"FUN" FUND		

Choose Your Investing Ratio

Begin earning and investing early in your . . . life. That will enable you to outpace the wealth accumulation levels of even the so-called gifted kids from your high school class.

—THOMAS J. STANLEY AND WILLIAM D. DANKO, *THE MILLIONAIRE NEXT DOOR*

As your future investment fund accumulates money, you can begin applying Mechanism 4. There are many ways to invest your money, including the stock market, real estate, bonds, commodities, crypto-currencies, and others. Because you're a FI Freak, you'll begin with the two strategies that have proved successful time and time again—index funds and real estate.

Since you are now 18, you can legally open a brokerage account and start investing in index funds, and you should! The next task will walk you through opening a brokerage account. First, however, you should decide how much money in your future investment fund will go toward index fund investing and how much will go toward real estate. The choice is yours; there is no correct answer, as both investments are proven strategies.

Typically, investing in real estate takes a back seat to stock market investing. This isn't because investing in the stock market is better, but because people think investing in real estate is complicated and difficult. Many think only the rich and savvy can invest in real estate. This is *false*. Anyone can invest in real estate—even a young FI Freak!

This workbook will set you on a path to buy your first real estate property in Freak Phase 12. If you're going to college, you'll do this during the second semester of your sophomore year. For this to happen, some of the money in your future investment fund must be earmarked for that first property purchase.

It's impossible to know today how much you'll need to save for your first property purchase. The amount will depend largely on the local real estate market where you buy your first property. If it is a very expensive market, you'll need to save more money.

Despite this uncertainty, you need to decide what percentage of your future investment fund will be for index fund investing and what percentage will be for future REI. That way you can start investing in index funds as soon as possible. Keep in mind that you can change your investment ratio over time—it is by no means set in stone.

If you have no preference or no clue as to what your investing ratio should be, start with a 50/50 split. This means that you will invest 50 percent of all deposits into your future investment fund in index funds, while the other half will sit in the account until the day you purchase your first property.

My Investing Ratio

INDEX FUNDS   REAL ESTATE

%   %

Open a Brokerage Account

A low-cost index fund is the most sensible equity investment for the great majority of investors... By periodically investing in an index fund, the know-nothing investor can actually out-perform most investment professionals.

—WARREN BUFFETT, QUOTED IN JOHN C. BOGLE, *THE LITTLE BOOK OF COMMON SENSE INVESTING*

Once you have some money in your future investment fund and some of it is earmarked for index fund investing, it's time to begin working on Mechanism 4! To invest in an index fund, you'll need to open a brokerage account. I go over the steps to opening a brokerage account toward the end of Chapter Twenty-Three in *First to a Million,* where I also list some index fund choices. (Those choices were current as of the writing of that book. You should ask a brokerage representative if they are still valid.) Review that section of Chapter Twenty-Three now. One important reminder from that chapter: Any money you invest in an index fund should be for the long term—at least ten years.

To open a brokerage account, first choose a brokerage firm. I list some of the large national firms in Chapter Twenty-Three. It is possible to open a brokerage account on most firms' websites without any assistance, but I recommend getting some help since you may have questions. Once you have decided which firm you want to use, call that firm and make an appointment to meet with a representative. That meeting can be in person or over the phone. In addition, try to find a parent or a trusted adult to help you open your brokerage account. A representative from the brokerage firm will walk you through the process, but it is still helpful to have an experienced adult there with you.

Once you have opened your account, you'll want to link your future investment savings account to your brokerage account so you can easily transfer money from one to the other. Be aware that when you transfer money into your brokerage account, it is *not* automatically invested. Your money will sit idle as "cash" until you actually invest it in a specific index fund.

If you have a steady income stream into your checking account, you can set up an automatic recurring transfer of money into your brokerage account. However, this is a good idea *only* if you have a steady income stream every month. For most teenagers, this is not the case.

If you do have a steady income stream (or once you do), follow these steps:
- Set up a recurring automatic transfer for a specified amount of money from your checking account (where your money comes in) to your future investment savings account every month. You can set up the recurring auto transfer on the bank's website. If you need help, talk to a trusted adult or a representative at your bank.

- Next, set up an auto transfer from your future investment savings account into your brokerage account every month. Remember, the amount you transfer should align with your investing ratio for index funds versus real estate. You can set up the recurring auto transfer on your brokerage firm's website. If you need help, talk to a trusted adult or a representative at the brokerage firm.

- Lastly, set up a recurring investment from your brokerage account into your chosen index fund every month. You can do this on your brokerage firm's website. If you need help, talk to a trusted adult or a representative at the brokerage firm.

This is how the process might work once you have everything set up, for a hypothetical monthly paycheck of $1,000:

- On the first of every month, your employer deposits your paycheck (steady income stream) into your checking account via direct deposit. The amount of your paycheck is pretty consistent and is around $1,000 per month. Some employers deposit biweekly ($500 every two weeks) or even weekly ($250 per week), but for the sake of this example, let's assume you are paid monthly.

- On the fifth of every month, your bank automatically transfers $500 from your checking account into your future investment savings account because you set up a recurring auto transfer.

- On the tenth of every month, your brokerage firm automatically transfers $250 (assuming your investing ratio is 50/50) from your future investment savings account into your brokerage account because you set up a recurring auto transfer.

- On the fifteenth of every month, your brokerage firm automatically invests $250 in your chosen index fund because you set up a recurring monthly investment.

As you can see, if you do not have a steady income stream, this system will not work for you. Instead, you'll need to complete all your transactions manually, using the apps on your phone. The first couple of times you do this, you may need help. But after a while, it should be quick and easy. Just remember to allow a few days between each transfer for processing.

✚ If you'll be transferring funds and investing manually on your phone's apps, put a RECURRING REMINDER in your calendar to transfer and invest any earmarked money into your chosen index fund every month.

For more information about index fund investing and the 4 Percent Rule, read the blog post at biggerpockets.com/teenworkbook.

TASK	NOTES	DATE COMPLETED
Choose the brokerage firm you will use and contact them.	Make an appointment to open your account at a time you can have a trusted adult present with you.	
Open your brokerage account		
Download the brokerage firm's app		
Set up auto transfer from checking to savings	If you have a steady income stream.	
Set up auto transfer from savings to brokerage	If you have a steady income stream.	
Set up recurring investment	If you have a steady income stream.	
Use apps to transfer and invest for the first time	If you *do not* have a steady income stream. Remember to allow a few days between each transaction for processing.	

FREAK PHASE *Five*

SEPTEMBER-DECEMBER
First semester of senior year of high school

Luck is the last dying wish of those who want to believe that winning can happen by accident. Hard work is for those who know it's a choice.

—UNKNOWN

Here is the checklist for this four-month Freak Phase. It's best to read the entire Freak Phase before filling in the due date for each item. Don't forget to use your calendar to help you stay on track. And remember—you're a FI Freak, so you've got this!

DUE DATES   ✓   TASK

○ Read *The House Hacking Strategy* by Craig Curelop.

○ Decide on your post-high school plans.

○ If you are pursuing postsecondary education, decide what that will look like.

○ If you are going to college, start applying for one scholarship per week.

○ Start narrowing down possible career paths or jobs.

○ Continue to learn about real estate investing.

○ Set three financial goals.

○ Implement a new Freak Tweak.

○ Sell a personal item you no longer need or want.

○ Find and do a new fun, free activity.

○ Interview someone who is where you want to be.

○ Evaluate your income streams.

○ Calculate and track your net worth.

○ Continue networking.

○ Shadow someone for a day.

+ACTION STEPS

DATE: _____

The date I communicated my three goals to my accountability partner.

Write out your three goals for this Freak Phase here.

① ....

② ....

③ ....

MY NEW "PAY YOURSELF FIRST"
PERCENTAGE GOAL IS: %

MY NEW
SAVINGS RATE GOAL IS: %

INTERVIEW Log

MONTH 1 / DATE COMPLETED

....

PERSON TO INTERVIEW

....

MONTH 2 / DATE COMPLETED

....

PERSON TO INTERVIEW

....

MONTH 3 / DATE COMPLETED

....

PERSON TO INTERVIEW

....

MONTH 4 / DATE COMPLETED

....

PERSON TO INTERVIEW

....

My New FREAK Tweak

FOR FRUGALITY IS...

Fun AND FREE Activity

✚ Put a **RECURRING REMINDER** in your calendar to complete these tasks at the
✚ beginning of every Freak Phase.

Read *The House Hacking Strategy* by Craig Curelop

House hacking is the most advantageous way to buy a first . . . property . . . It allows the owner to live for free or at exceptionally low cost, while others pay rents covering [the owner's] mortgage payment. This is the way to turn one's housing expenses into a wealth creation tool.

—SCOTT TRENCH, *SET FOR LIFE*

Craig is *the* expert on the house hacking strategy, which is by far the best strategy for young real estate investors to get started. As you'll read in his book, he *maximized* the house hacking strategy to achieve FI in just four years!

FREAK TECHNIQUE

HOUSE HACKING: An REI strategy in which you live in one of the units or rooms of your property while renting out the other units or rooms, using your tenants' rents to pay your mortgage and expenses.

 One of the reasons house hacking is so powerful is because it can eliminate your largest expense: housing. In Chapter Eighteen in *First to a Million*, we went over the three largest expenses for most people: housing, transportation, and food. Housing is number one. Eliminating the largest expense in your life is a complete game changer. It helps you dominate Mechanism 2, which will help you crush Mechanisms 3 and 4, getting you to early FI *very* quickly.

 As you read Craig's book, pay special attention to Chapter Five, which covers financing. Take notes and highlight stuff in this chapter so you can easily return to the main points. In the next Phase, we will begin exploring the options for financing your first property. Chapter Five of *The House Hacking Strategy* is a great introduction to those options.

 Visit biggerpockets.com/teenworkbook for some important YouTube links to videos about house hacking.

Decide on Your Post-High School Plans

I know, I know. It's too early for you to decide what you want to do after high school. But I would urge you to make a general decision by the end of this Phase (end of the semester). Deciding where you are headed will allow you to move forward with some other decisions. At this point, you don't have to decide which college you are going to, what job you'll get, or where you'll move. Those are decisions for the next Phase.

For now, try to decide which of these four options you'll pursue after graduation:

1. Continue your education
2. Enter the job force
3. Enter the military
4. Take a gap year

While you contemplate this big decision, I recommend you look over Chapter Twenty-Six in *First to a Million*, which walks you through the pros and cons of the "college or no college" decision.

In that chapter, I discuss the one significant disadvantage of going to college full-time in relation to REI. To invest in real estate, you should be able to qualify for a mortgage. Without a mortgage, buying property is difficult. (There are other ways to get it done, but I'm keeping things simple for now.) To qualify for a mortgage, you'll need verifiable income from a W-2 job. This is because the bank wants to make sure you can make your mortgage payment on time every month.

Most college students hit a snag here. If someone is in school full-time, they can't work a full-time job. And without one to two years of verifiable income from a full-time job, that student won't qualify for a mortgage.

There is one workaround many young people can use. That is to have a trusted adult (usually a parent) co-sign on the mortgage. If you have a co-signer, the bank will consider their income history (and their credit score) with the mortgage application. Usually, this allows the mortgage to be approved and the purchase to go through. But not all young people have that option, which is why I am telling you about the W-2 income snag now.

If you decide to go to college, you may very well have to postpone your first real estate purchase until a couple of years after graduation. Again, there are ways to make it happen, but they are less common than traditional mortgage purchases. Some of you will be comfortable with waiting to make your first purchase. Others may want it to happen as soon as possible. So keep this information in mind while considering your post–high school options.

I do have some good news. No matter what your plans are after high school, you can continue to invest in index funds with no strings attached (as long as you must have the money to invest).

OF THE FOUR POST—HIGH SCHOOL
OPTIONS ABOVE, I WILL:

If You Are Pursuing Postsecondary Education, Decide What That Will Look Like

I'm going to push you a bit more when it comes to your plans after high school. If you intend to continue your education after high school, try to decide what that will look like. Here are the most common options:

- Attend a four-year college or university
- Attend a community college
- Attend an online school
- Enroll in an associate program
- Participate in an apprenticeship
- Complete a trade or certificate program

I cover many of these options in Chapter Twenty-Seven of *First to a Million*. I recommend reviewing those discussions if you need more information.

If you'll be continuing your education after high school, which of these options will you choose?

IF I SEEK CONTINUING EDUCATION AFTER HIGH
SCHOOL, I WILL:

If You Are Going to College, Apply for One Scholarship a Week

If you choose to go to college after high school, start applying for scholarships *now*. I list numerous resources in Appendix B of *First to a Million* that will help you complete this task. Review those resources and start making your own list of scholarships to apply for. Keep track of the ones you apply for and the due dates for others. Follow up on applications when needed. You may use the form below or create your own in a Google Sheet or something similar.

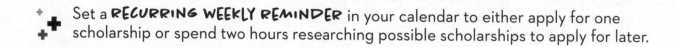 Set a **RECURRING WEEKLY REMINDER** in your calendar to either apply for one scholarship or spend two hours researching possible scholarships to apply for later.

NAME OF SCHOLARSHIP	SCHOLARSHIP AMOUNT	DUE DATE FOR APPLICATION	DATE I SUBMITTED MY APPLICATION	RESULT/DATE TO FOLLOW UP

Start Narrowing Down Possible Career Paths or Jobs

This task applies to all of you. For those of you who will be continuing your education, you'll need to pick an area of study or a major very soon. If you are headed to college, review the section titled "Pick a Promising Major" in Chapter Twenty-Seven of *First to a Million*. For those of you who will start working full-time right after high school graduation, this task has immediate importance.

If you have no idea what kind of career or job you want after high school, I'd like to throw out a couple of options for you to consider. Both will provide you with ample time off to pursue other endeavors, such as developing a side hustle, building a business, or investing in real estate. Both require some additional school or training but can usually be done in less than four years. And they both happen to be service-based jobs that can be very rewarding and fulfilling. However, these ideas are just to get you thinking. You should ultimately choose a job or career you are highly interested in for your own reasons.

Firefighter

What you might not know about firefighting is that it lends itself very well to pursuing early FI. One reason is that you can earn a pretty good income without a college education. But the greatest benefit is that many firehouses will require you to work two 24-hour shifts a week, allowing you plenty of time to pursue other endeavors during your time off.

Research your local area to see how much competition there is for these positions and what it takes to get hired. It may be beneficial to get some post-secondary education relevant to being a firefighter. For example, in California it is possible to get a two-year degree in fire technology. Becoming an EMT (Emergency Medical Technician) before applying to be a firefighter can also be helpful. This will require about 120 to 150 hours of coursework, and you'll have to pass a test when you're done. As part of your research, start using your new networking skills to set up an interview or shadowing experience with a firefighter in your area.

Please do *not* become a firefighter if your only reason is wanting a flexible schedule to have an easier path to FI. However, if you legitimately believe you would like to serve your community in this capacity, firefighting could be a practical option for you.

Nurse

If you have already considered nursing as a career, you should know it can have additional benefits for a young person pursuing early FI. Those benefits are maximized if you choose to be a traveling nurse.

A traveling nurse moves to different cities taking nursing jobs at hospitals that need extra help. As a traveling nurse, you'll typically work three 12-hour shifts per week, giving you four days off to pursue other endeavors, such as a side hustle or business venture. You'll also get paid up to twice what a typical nurse would make. In addition, traveling nurses receive a housing stipend to help pay for their living arrangements for their temporary stay in a new city—typically six weeks to four months long. The housing stipends can be around $2,000 per month. And if you don't spend all of it on housing, you get to keep the difference!

Nurses can also often pick up extra shifts, thus working overtime (more than forty hours per week) and making overtime pay (typically 1.5 times the average pay), which can significantly boost your income as well. (Working overtime could be your "side hustle.") Add all this together, and a frugal traveling nurse can make a very significant income.

Now the bad news. To be a traveling nurse, you generally need a four-year degree. However, motivated students can complete their program in three years or even fewer. In addition, you would likely need two years of experience as a nurse after obtaining your degree to begin working as a traveling nurse. While the benefits of being a traveling nurse are great, they are also down the road a few years.

Again, please do *not* become a nurse just because of the flexible schedule and income perks. It is an extremely tough job that will only be enjoyable if you have a genuine passion for it.

Write down information here about your most likely future job or career options:

JOB/CAREER	EDUCATION NEEDED	TYPICAL ANNUAL INCOME FOR A NEW EMPLOYEE	HOW COMPETITIVE IS THIS JOB MARKET?

Continue to Learn About Real Estate Investing

Real estate is by far the fastest path to FI. Hands down.

—GRANT SABATIER, *BIGGERPOCKETS MONEY PODCAST*, EPISODE 58

There are many different types of real estate properties you can buy as an investment. Here is a list of the most common:
- Single-family homes (SFH)
- Townhouses or condos

- Small multifamily properties with four units or fewer (duplexes, triplexes, and fourplexes)
- Large multifamily properties with more than four units
- Mobile home parks
- Commercial real estate

There are also many strategies you can use when investing. Here is a list of the most common:
- Long-term buy and hold
- Short-term rental (Airbnb and VRBO, for example)
- House hacking
- Fix and flip (also known as flipping)
- Live-in fix and flip
- BRRRR (buy, rehab, rent, refinance, repeat)
- Out-of-state investing
- Turnkey investing

I highly recommend house hacking as the way to begin your REI career. It is by far the best strategy for young investors.

A live-in fix and flip is another excellent option for young investors. It's even possible—though not necessarily easy—to combine house hacking with a live-in fix and flip.

With some planning, you can also make your investment more profitable by working a short-term rental into your house hack.

You'll be learning about all these types of real estate properties and investing strategies while working your way through the workbook. I'm mentioning these now so you can start to do your own research if you're excited about REI. YouTube and BiggerPockets are great places to start learning the basics.

Visit biggerpockets.com/teenworkbook for some important links to podcasts and YouTube videos about these REI strategies.

Congratulations! You've just completed Freak Phase 5! It's time to be proud of your Freakishness and check in with your progress. Post a video of yourself describing the three most meaningful tasks you completed in this Freak Phase, and post a picture of yourself with your completed checklist from the beginning of this Phase. Don't forget to use **#FREAKPHASE5** and **#TEENAGEFIFREAK** and to tag **@SHEEKSFREAKS** and **@BIGGERPOCKETS!**

JANUARY–APRIL

Second semester of senior year of high school

Success is doing what you want to do, when you want, where you want, with whom you want, as much as you want.

—TONY ROBBINS

Here is the checklist for this four-month Freak Phase. It's best to read the entire Freak Phase before filling in the due date for each item. Don't forget to use your calendar to help you stay on track. And remember—you're a FI Freak, so you've got this!

DUE DATES	✓	TASK
	◯	Read *Your Money or Your Life* by Vicki Robin and Joe Dominguez.
	◯	Get involved with your family's income taxes.
	◯	Finalize plans for after high school.
	◯	Decide on housing for after high school.
	◯	Make a plan/budget for income and expenses after high school.
	◯	If you are going to college, apply for two scholarships a week.
	◯	Start building a steady W-2 income history.
	◯	Continue to learn about real estate investing.
	◯	Set three financial goals.
	◯	Implement a new Freak Tweak.
	◯	Sell a personal item you no longer need or want.
	◯	Find and do a new fun, free activity.
	◯	Interview someone who is where you want to be.
	◯	Evaluate your income streams.
	◯	Calculate and track your net worth.
	◯	Continue networking.
	◯	Shadow someone for a day.

Goals

+ACTION STEPS

DATE: _____

The date I communicated my three goals to my accountability partner.

Write out your three goals for this Freak Phase here.

1 ....

2 ....

3 ....

MY NEW "PAY YOURSELF FIRST"
PERCENTAGE
GOAL IS: %

MY NEW
SAVINGS RATE
GOAL IS: %

MONTH 1 / DATE COMPLETED

....

PERSON TO INTERVIEW

....

MONTH 2 / DATE COMPLETED

....

PERSON TO INTERVIEW

....

MONTH 3 / DATE COMPLETED

....

PERSON TO INTERVIEW

....

MONTH 4 / DATE COMPLETED

....

PERSON TO INTERVIEW

....

FOR FRUGALITY IS...

Put a **RECURRING REMINDER** in your calendar to complete these tasks at the beginning of every Freak Phase.

Read *Your Money or Your Life*

Your Money or Your Life, by Vicki Robin and Joe Dominguez, is widely regarded as one of the keystone books about early FI. First published in 1992, it's been updated twice since then. Read this groundbreaking book and take notes!

Get Involved with Your Family's Income Taxes

It's the beginning of the year, and that means it's income tax season. Every individual or family in the United States must file their income tax return for a given year by April 15th of the following year. This means your family will be going through this process very soon, if not now. You have an opportunity to learn more about your family's finances and how income taxes work by getting involved in the process.

Talk to a parent about being engaged in your family's income tax return preparation. You've already been helping to pay the family bills every month, and now it's time to level up. Your family might prepare their own tax returns, or they might hire someone to do it for them. In either case, you should be part of the process.

As a teenager who is earning some income, you may or may not need to file a separate tax return from your parents. There are numerous tax laws and options, and they are constantly changing. Therefore, I recommend you and your family hire a professional to help you with your taxes. A professional can look at your entire family's situation and give you advice for your best outcome. (And they will also make sure you follow the law, which is a good thing!) There will come a point when you file your own separate tax return. It could be this year, or it could be in the near future. Again, ask your tax professional when it would be best to start filing your own returns.

 Set a **RECURRING REMINDER** in your calendar to file your income tax return every **FEBRUARY.**

✓	TASK
○	Talk to a parent about helping with the family's tax return this year.
○	Help your parent collect and organize the necessary documents.
○	Help your parent complete your family's income tax return and ask them any questions you may have.
○	If your family decides to hire a professional to help with the tax return, ask the professional when and why you should start filing your own taxes.
○	If your family had a professional do your taxes, look over the finished forms and ask the professional any questions you may have.

Finalize Plans for After High School

In the last Phase, you decided which of these options you would pursue after high school:

1. Continue your education
2. Enter the job force
3. Enter the military
4. Take a gap year

Now that you're in your last semester of high school, it's time to decide *exactly* what you'll do. Give this decision the consideration it deserves. I highly recommend you also review Chapters Twenty-Six and Twenty-Seven in *First to a Million*.

Let's explore each of these four options a little more.

Continue Your Education

You now need to decide what *type* of school to attend. Will you choose a traditional four-year school, a community college, a technical school, an online school, or something else? (I go over the pros and cons of these options in Chapter Twenty-Seven of *First to a Million*.) You also need to decide *which* school you'll attend.

The critical piece to this decision is financing, because how you pay for school will affect your future. My best advice is this: Do *everything* you can to avoid *all* student loan debt. This may very well mean choosing a path that is not normal. But *you* are not normal. You are a FI Freak! Doing things differently is how you thrive.

Enter The Job Force

This option involves getting a job right after graduating from high school. As you know, this gives you a financial advantage over the college route because you can begin working full-time right away. You can further maximize Mechanism 1 by getting a second, part-time job or by building a side hustle or small business. You can even use your nights and weekends to build marketable skills through online classes, tutorials, in-person classes, or research. Without having to dedicate massive amounts of time to classes as a full-time student, you can fast-forward your journey to FI.

The downside is that you may not be able to get the job you want without a college degree. Also, you may not earn a high salary from your full-time job right out of high school. With the right college degree, you could earn two or three times as much, albeit a few years down the road.

In Chapter Twenty-Six, I list several high-paying jobs that do not require a four-year degree. Maybe you'll pursue one of these. Perhaps there's a side hustle you'd like to devote all your time to. Or maybe you'll choose another excellent option, such as website developer, handyperson, door-to-door salesperson, or real estate agent. Whatever your choice, make sure you have a plan in place before you walk across that stage to get your diploma.

Enter The Military

If this is your chosen path, then first, I want to thank you for deciding to serve our country. I wish you a safe and adventurous military career, whether it be for two years or thirty.

Serving in the military has some fantastic benefits that can help a FI Freak reach their goals. Your expenses are greatly diminished, as the military almost always takes care of housing and food—two of your three largest expenses! Also, you'll have a steady income, even if it may not be considerable. That income, along with low living expenses, can help you when you choose to buy your first house hack property.

One of the young people I work with is in the Marines and stationed in South Carolina. His name is Jabbar, and he is a full-fledged FI Freak. He bought his first property (a four-bedroom house hack) at age 19! At the same time, he was investing in index funds and working a couple of side hustles, including driving for Door Dash. He made frugal choices. And he is now crushing life as FI Freak.

See biggerpockets.com/teenworkbook for a link to a series of YouTube videos, made by Marine and fellow FI Freak Jabbar, documenting his journey to his first house hack.

Take A Gap Year

There are several reasons for taking a gap year before heading to college or getting a long-term job. For instance:

- You want to engage in some service or volunteer work.
- You want to travel and explore.
- You want to try out a career field for a short time.
- You want to focus on a side hustle for a year to see what may happen.

Whatever your reason may be, this is an excellent choice. Even if taking a gap year prolongs your journey to early FI, you'll be rewarded with unforgettable experiences and additional wisdom. Life is meant to be lived, and a gap year gives you a chance to do just that.

One warning, however: Do *not* rack up debt to fund your gap year. This can be as damaging to your financial future as student loans, car loans, or other consumer debt. If doing a gap year, plan to do it *without* borrowing money.

Real Estate–Related Jobs

At this point, you may be highly interested in real estate as a means of building wealth *and* as a potential income-earning job. If so, this is an excellent time to go over some jobs in the real estate world.

Keep in mind that if you are seeking one of these jobs straight out of high school (or even straight out of college), you may need to start as an assistant or a trainee before advancing to some of the jobs below. But if you are hardworking, dependable, and eager to learn, your assistant stint should not last too long.

By taking a job related to real estate, you are doing what Robert Kiyosaki calls "working to learn, not to earn." That is, you are learning things that can help you in your future endeavors while earning a paycheck at the same time—but the main benefit is what you learn, not what you earn. Here is a list of some real estate–related jobs for young people. I will also list the education or training needed for each.

- Real estate agent: An agent helps clients buy and sell real estate. You'll need a real estate license from the state in which you want to work.

- Real estate broker: A broker is an agent who has also passed the broker license exam, which qualifies them to own a real estate firm and hire agents to work for them.

- Real estate agent/broker assistant: While getting your real estate license, why not work in an agent/broker's office as an assistant to get your foot in the door and learn as much as you can? No license or degree is needed.

- Real estate appraiser trainee: A real estate appraiser estimates the market value of real estate before important events, such as a sale. The appraisal industry is regulated differently in each state, but most states require you to start your career as a trainee before becoming a licensed residential appraiser. To become a trainee, you must complete and pass specific coursework.

- Property manager assistant: Property management companies employ assistants to help property managers oversee a variety of property types. Some standard duties include handling marketing campaigns, showing properties to prospective tenants, addressing tenant complaints, and fulfilling maintenance requests. No certification or classwork is needed to be an assistant. However, most states require a license to become a property manager.

- Mortgage loan officer: Loan officers help people secure financing for real estate purchases or investments. They may specialize in mortgage, commercial, or consumer loans. You'll need a license or certification.

MY SPECIFIC PLANS FOR AFTER HIGH SCHOOL ARE:

Decide on Housing for After High School

In Chapter Eighteen in *First to a Million*, we went over the three most likely living situations after graduating from high school. They are:
1. Continue to live at home
2. Live in a dorm or other school housing
3. Rent a place to live

In that chapter, I talk about each of these options. Go back and review that information if needed.

One option I did not touch on was renting a room in a house that someone *else* is house hacking. You may not be quite ready to do your own house hack yet, but that doesn't mean you can't take advantage of the strategy now. Obviously, you should make your selection very carefully. But doing this can save you thousands of dollars over the course of a year. It's just one more way to be frugal and maximize Mechanism 2. You may even learn a thing or two from the owner-landlord while you're living there!

<table>
<tr><td>MY SPECIFIC
PLANS FOR
HOUSING
AFTER HIGH SCHOOL ARE:</td><td></td></tr>
</table>

Make a Plan/Budget for Income and Expenses After High School

The cost of [your] lifestyle will be the single largest determinant of when [you] achieve early financial freedom.

—SCOTT TRENCH, *SET FOR LIFE*

Graduating from high school is an exciting accomplishment. There are many different ways one can proceed from this point. But even if you are going to continue living at home, you'll likely have a change in your financial responsibilities.

Therefore, it's time to take a fresh new look at what your projected income and expenses will be after graduation. You'll likely need to account for some new monthly bills. Will you now be responsible for your cell phone? How about your car insurance, food, or clothing? Have a discussion with your parents about what they expect you to pay for once you graduate from high school.

If you are moving out, you'll face some decisions: Should you pay for your own Netflix account? What about health insurance? Should you get your own cell phone plan? (I recommend asking your parents if you can stay on their account but pay them your share of the monthly bill. It will be far less expensive than having your own account.)

Once you know your plans after high school, where you'll live, and what expenses your parents will continue to help you with, you'll have a much clearer picture of your projected income and expenses. Now it's time to list everything out.

Use the following chart as a starting point. Eventually, make a budget in your tracking app. The expense listed first in this chart is "pay yourself first." You'll use this money to support your FI Freak journey by funding all three of your savings accounts. If your total income is greater than your total expenses, you'll have more money to save. If your total expenses are higher, you'll need to adjust your other expenses (not "pay yourself first") to balance your budget.

MY NEW "AFTER HIGH SCHOOL" MONTHLY BUDGET

INCOME		EXPENSES (some may not apply)	
Full-time job		Pay yourself first	
Part-time job		Tuition	
Side hustle no. 1		School supplies	
Side hustle no. 2		Rent	
Gifts received		Food	
Passive income		Clothing	
(List more below)		Transportation	
		Entertainment	
		Utilities	
		Cell phone	
		Gifts	
		Subscriptions	
		Memberships	
		Health and beauty	
		Pets	
		Travel	
		(List more below)	
TOTAL INCOME:		TOTAL EXPENSES:	

If You Are Going to College, Apply for Two Scholarships a Week

Those of you who are heading to college started applying for one scholarship every week in the last Phase. It's time to level that up to two per week. Remember, there are numerous resources in Appendix B of *First to a Million* that will help you complete this task. Go through the entire list and start making your own list of possible scholarships to apply for. Be keeping track of the ones you've applied for and the due dates for others in this workbook, as well as in a Google Sheet or something similar. Don't forget to follow up on applications as needed.

✚ Set a **RECURRING WEEKLY REMINDER** in your calendar to apply for two scholarships.

NAME OF SCHOLARSHIP	SCHOLARSHIP AMOUNT	DUE DATE FOR APPLICATION	DATE I SUBMITTED MY APPLICATION	RESULT/DATE TO FOLLOW UP

Start Building a Steady W-2 Income History

It doesn't take that many properties to achieve financial freedom. It just takes the right ones.

—BRANDON TURNER, *3 STEPS TO FINANCIAL FREEDOM (IN 10 YEARS OR LESS!) (WEBINAR)*, WWW.BIGGERPOCKETS.COM

The *First to a Million* workbook will guide you toward purchasing your first real estate property (a house hack) in two years—during Freak Phase 12. For most of you, that will be a best-case scenario; some of you might not make your first purchase until a few years after that. Nonetheless, I'm laying out the best-case scenario so that all of you can see what needs to happen before you make that purchase. FI Freaks who will not be full-time students are the most likely to achieve this best-case scenario. It will be more difficult for full-time students—but it's not impossible!

Earlier in this Phase, you wrote down exactly what you'll do after high school. I wanted you to think about that first so this task would not interfere with your answer. The decision about what path you'll pursue after high school is personal, and there is no right or wrong answer. Your desire or plan to invest in real estate should have a minimal role, if any, in that decision. For example, I would *not* recommend passing on a college degree *only* because doing so will make it easier to buy a house hack property four years sooner.

With that said, I will be explaining the following options for both a full-time student and a full-time worker. Read through this task carefully as we explore the critical strategies *all* FI Freaks should use to buy their first property as soon as they can.

The Most Common Roadblock

Generally, you'll need four things to buy your first property. They are:

1. Knowledge
2. Cash
3. Excellent credit score
4. Steady income

If you follow this workbook, the first three items on the list should not be an issue. It's the fourth one that presents a challenge for most young aspiring real estate investors.

In Chapter Five of *The House Hacking Strategy*, Craig Curelop explains many ways to finance (pay for) a property to house hack. I asked you to take notes or highlight important information in that chapter.

By far the most common loans (mortgages) to finance a property with are conventional loans and FHA loans. (This is the good debt I discuss in Chapter Ten of *First to a Million*.) These two types of loans are very similar, and since they are the most popular ways to buy a first property, I will focus on them.

The information presented in this workbook about mortgage qualifications should not be considered absolute. The mortgage industry changes over time, and requirements tighten or loosen depending on many factors. Regardless, it comes down to this: A lender will not loan you money to buy a property unless they are very confident you can pay them back. They will want you to show them you have enough steady, verifiable income to make those payments. If you are a full-time student, this won't be easy because you probably don't have a full-time job.

The Co-Signer

For those who don't have steady, verifiable income, one fantastic solution is to have a trusted adult (most likely a parent) co-sign on the mortgage with you. That way, the bank will look at both your income and the co-signer's. If one of your parents has a steady income, you may qualify for the loan without having any income of your own. The flip side is that your co-signer is taking a massive risk. If you don't make the mortgage payments, the co-signer must do it for you.

FREAK SPEAK

FS

CO-SIGNER/CO-BORROWER: Someone who signs a mortgage with a real estate buyer when the buyer does not have sufficient income history or credit score. The income history of the co-signer or co-borrower can satisfy the lender's income requirements. Co-signers don't co-own the property, while co-borrowers do.

However, not all of you will have an adult who is willing to do this for you. If that's the case, don't give up on this solution just yet. Remember, the goal is to buy a property in two years. So even if you don't have any adults in your life who would be willing to co-sign on a mortgage *today*, that doesn't mean they won't co-sign when you actually need them to. You have *two years* to change their mind!

Make it a point to continuously update them on what you are learning and accomplishing. Tell them about your side hustles, your Freakish frugality techniques, and your goal of living for free in a house hack. Explain to them how a house hack works by showing them the numbers. Answer their questions with confident, well-thought-out answers. Convince them you *can* do this so they will eventually agree to help you out by co-signing on that mortgage. You may even share some of the cash flow with them or bring them in as a 50/50 partner. Get creative! A FI Freak doesn't say "I can't." They say "How can I?"

Why Are We Talking About This Now?

As I said before, the workbook will guide you toward buying your first house hack property in two years. We're talking about this now because two years is the typical amount of time a lender will analyze when looking over your income history. They will want to see two years of income without any gaps.

If you cannot find a co-signer when the time comes, it becomes your responsibility to prove you can make the payments to your lender. And if they are going to look at your income history over the past two years, you'll need a job that counts.

A job that "counts" is a W-2 job. This is a job where you work for someone else, and they pay you regularly from their business's account. It's not when a neighbor pays you to take care of their house or do some yard work. It's most likely not any of your side hustles. And it's not passive income. It's a regular job where you make a certain amount per hour and show up to work when scheduled.

You'll know you are working a W-2 job because you'll have to fill out a W-4 tax form when you begin working. If you have any doubts about whether a job is a W-2 job, ask the employer.

W-2 TAX FORM: The IRS form an employer is required to send to each employee and the IRS at the end of the year that lists how much money the employee made that year.

 W-4 TAX FORM: The IRS form *you* complete to let your employer know how much money to withhold from your paycheck for federal taxes.

Full-Time Worker (Including College Graduates)

This is the best situation to be in if you want to buy your first property in two years. You'll simply need to get a full-time job as soon as you can. But there are some catches. You must work for the same employer for two years in order to secure a mortgage. (You can change jobs, just not employers.) And the job must pay well enough (or should eventually) that you can afford to buy a house.

If you have had your full-time job for at least two years and it pays enough to meet the required debt-to-income ratio, you'll have a good chance of being approved for a mortgage, even without a co-signer.

The process will be even easier if you get a full-time *salaried* job. In that case, you may only need to have a few months of work history with your employer, not two years.

Full-Time Student

This is the more difficult path if you want to buy your first real estate property in two years without a co-signer. The only way you'll qualify for a mortgage is to have a two-year history of part-time employment with an average income high enough to meet the required debt-to-income ratio. (I am assuming a full-time student would not also be a full-time worker.)

You will still need to have a job with the same employer for at least two years. The lender will average your paychecks, and there shouldn't be any gaps or significant changes in the number of hours worked. Your income should be "steady." (It can actually look bad if you change to full-time in the summer.)

You can be a full-time student and work a part-time job over the next two years. The challenge is earning a high enough average income to meet the required debt-to-income ratio.

Debt-To-Income Ratio

A lender will also want to see that you have a good debt-to-income (DTI) ratio before they lend to you. They will look at your gross income (income before taxes are taken out) from a consistent W-2 job. The "debt" number is how much money you pay toward debt, such as mortgages, credit cards, car loans, and student loans. (In the following calculations, we'll assume you won't have any debt payments other than the mortgage you are seeking—which should be true!)

 DEBT-TO-INCOME (DTI) RATIO: All your monthly debt payments divided by your gross monthly income; the lower the ratio, the better.

Each lender will have slightly different ratios they will accept for different applicants, and those ratios can change over time. For this example, we will assume the applicant needs a DTI ratio of 30 percent or lower.

Let's also assume you are working full-time for $20 an hour, which comes to a gross monthly income of roughly $3,200. You want to buy a house for $200,000 and plan on putting 5 percent down, which is $10,000. Therefore, you'll need to borrow $190,000. With a 4 percent interest rate, your monthly payments for that mortgage would be around $900. Therefore, your DTI would be:

$900 ÷ $3,200 = 28 percent

Great! Your DTI ratio is below 30 percent, so you should be good to go. (The lender will consider other factors too, but this is by far the biggest stumbling block for most young people.)

You can also use your gross income and the lender's DTI ratio requirement to see how much you would be able to borrow. Once you have that number, you can determine how expensive a property you can afford.

Let's assume you had the same job earning a gross income of $3,200 per month. You also know the lender requires a 30 percent DTI ratio or lower. To calculate your maximum monthly loan payment allowed by the lender, you would take your gross monthly income and multiply it by 30 percent. Therefore:

$3,200 × .30 = $960

That means $960 is the maximum monthly payment the lender will allow you to have for the mortgage. Under these conditions, the most expensive property you can afford is around $212,000.

What Now?

Take all of this into consideration—along with how soon you want to buy your first property—as you decide when to get a W-2 job. If you are adamant about following the workbook's strategy and buying your first property in two years, you now know how to give yourself the best chance at qualifying for a mortgage. If you are okay with waiting on that first real estate purchase, then getting a W-2 job now is not as important.

Finally, remember that there are other options. Getting a co-signer is a great one. Craig Curelop talks about others in Chapter Five of *The House Hacking Strategy*. Here we just focused on the most common way to buy a property.

Write out your plan regarding a W-2 job and getting approved for a mortgage by answering these questions:

Q. Will I be a full-time student or a full-time employee?
A.

Q. When do I want to buy my first real estate property?
A.

Q. Do I think I will be able to find a co-signer?

A.

Q. When do I want to start building up a consistent W-2 income history?

A.

Q. What is my estimated DTI ratio for the next year of my life?

A.

Continue to Learn About Real Estate Investing

Fix And Flips (Flipping)

There's a subset of real estate investors who make money by "flipping" properties: buying fixer-uppers, fixing them up, and selling them for a hefty profit. This may be a strategy for some FIers in their wealth accumulation phase, but it fails the test for an FI portfolio. There's too much work, too much risk.

—VICKI ROBIN AND JOE DOMINGUEZ, *YOUR MONEY OR YOUR LIFE*

The fix-and-flip strategy gets a lot of airtime on TV and a lot of attention in the REI world. TV shows can make this strategy look easy and incredibly profitable. But before you navigate down this path, I want to give you some more grounded information about flipping.

FIX AND FLIP (FLIPPING): Buying a distressed property, doing renovations or repairs, and then selling it at a higher price.

First off, it's not easy. Flipping can *get* easy once you've done it for a few years, but your first few attempts will be difficult. Second, a fix and flip can take months to complete. It might seem like it takes just a few weeks on a thirty-minute TV show, but that's not the case!

Third, and maybe most important, flipping is neither a passive income stream nor an investment that will build long-term wealth. It is a job. When you flip a house, you sell it at the end: That's when you earn money. And the house you just sold will never make you money again. Therefore, to make more money, you need to flip another house. Rental properties, on the other hand, are investments that continue to make money for you over a long period of time.

The Live-In Fix And Flip

A live-in fix and flip is different. As the name suggests, you'll actually live in the property while you fix it up, and you'll live there for at least two years. With this strategy, you benefit from having a place to live while you make the mortgage payment. This means you are saving rent on a separate place to live. (In a normal fix and flip, you are making payments on the money borrowed to buy the property, but no one is living there.)

 LIVE-IN FIX AND FLIP: Buying a distressed property, doing renovations or repairs while living in the property, and then selling it at a higher price at least two years later and avoiding capital gains tax.

There's also the massive benefit of no capital gains tax, which is why people do live-in fix and flips. To understand the enormity of this benefit, let's look at how taxes work for some real estate scenarios.

Let's say you did a normal fix and flip. You bought a property, fixed it up, and made $25,000 in profit. The government would tax that money.

Let's say you bought a house, fixed it up while living in it for a year, and then sold it. You also made $25,000. The government would tax that money too.

Now, let's say you bought a house, fixed it up while living in it for *two* years, and then sold it. Again, you made $25,000. The government would not charge you *any* tax. *Zero.* That can save you thousands of dollars! And that is why a live-in fix and flip can be such a profitable strategy. You have to live somewhere. Maybe a live-in fix and flip will be best for you.

The key is you must have lived in the property for at least two of the last five years when you sell it. If that is true, the law says you don't have to pay any tax. (There are some limitations, but they're pretty uncommon.) Technically, you could live in the property for the first two years while you are fixing it up, then rent it out for two years and eleven months, and sell it without having to pay tax on the gain. Now you're getting creative.

Some investors do live-in fix and flips and move every two years. Not a bad plan! You can still buy other investment properties while you're living in the fix and flip. But you can't do a house hack *and* a live-in fix and flip at the same time, because both strategies require you to live in the property.

You could, however, buy a fix and flip and live in it for two years while fixing it up. Then you could move into a new house hacking property while renting out the fix and flip for up to three years. That's two properties gaining you income. Now you're getting *really* creative!

You could also combine house hacking with a live-in fix and flip in the same property. You would live in it for two years (most house hackers stay for only one year) and do all the fixing up right away, before your tenants move in. Then you get the benefit of tax-free growth *and* low-cost or free housing. *Now you're getting really Freaking creative!*

CONGRATULATIONS!

You've just completed Freak Phase 6! It's time to be proud of your Freakishness and check in with your progress. Post a video of yourself describing the three most meaningful tasks you completed in this Freak Phase, and post a picture of yourself with your completed checklist from the beginning of this Phase.

Don't forget to use **#FREAKPHASE6** and **#TEENAGEFIFREAK** and to tag **@SHEEKSFREAKS** and **@BIGGERPOCKETS!**

FREAK PHASE Seven

MAY-AUGUST
Summer after high school graduation

A life spent in making mistakes is not only more honorable but more useful than a life spent doing nothing.

—GEORGE BERNARD SHAW

Here is the checklist for this four-month Freak Phase. It's best to read the entire Freak Phase before filling in the due date for each item. Don't forget to use your calendar to help you stay on track. And remember—you're a FI Freak, so you've got this!

DUE DATES	✓	TASK
	◯	Read *The Book on Rental Property Investing* by Brandon Turner.
	◯	Maximize your extra time this summer.
	◯	Talk to your parents about health insurance.
	◯	If you are going to college, choose your major wisely.
	◯	Manage your expenses after high school.
	◯	Start another passive income stream.
	◯	Continue investing in index funds.
	◯	Watch the documentary *Playing with FIRE*.
	◯	Continue to learn about real estate investing.
	◯	Set three financial goals.
	◯	Implement a new Freak Tweak.
	◯	Sell a personal item you no longer need or want.
	◯	Find and do a new fun, free activity.
	◯	Interview someone who is where you want to be.
	◯	Evaluate your income streams.
	◯	Calculate and track your net worth.
	◯	Continue networking.
	◯	Shadow someone for a day.

Goals + ACTION STEPS

The date I communicated my three goals to my accountability partner.

Write out your three goals for this Freak Phase here.

1 ....

2 ....

3 ....

MY NEW "PAY YOURSELF FIRST"
PERCENTAGE
GOAL IS: %

MY NEW
SAVINGS RATE
GOAL IS: %

INTERVIEW Log

MONTH 1 / DATE COMPLETED

....

PERSON TO INTERVIEW

....

MONTH 2 / DATE COMPLETED

....

PERSON TO INTERVIEW

....

MONTH 3 / DATE COMPLETED

....

PERSON TO INTERVIEW

....

MONTH 4 / DATE COMPLETED

....

PERSON TO INTERVIEW

....

My New FREAK Tweak
FOR FRUGALITY IS...

Put a **RECURRING REMINDER** in your calendar to complete these tasks at the beginning of every Freak Phase.

Read *The Book on Rental Property Investing* by Brandon Turner

This is one of the best-selling books on real estate investing. It covers every topic you need to know about at this point in your FI Freak journey. Pay close attention to Chapters Thirteen and Fourteen, which discuss financing and getting approved for a mortgage. This will add more information to what we discussed in the last Phase and help you get even more on track to securing a mortgage for your first property purchase. Also read Chapter Five carefully and take notes. This chapter explains how to analyze a property's numbers to see if it will be a good deal. We will cover this topic in more detail in the next Phase.

Maximize Your Extra Time This Summer

First, congratulations on your graduation from high school! I sincerely hope you had a great senior year and that you are now excited for the next chapter in your FI Freak journey. Graduating from high school is a significant milestone. I hope you are proud of your accomplishment and took the time to celebrate!

Now that you no longer must worry about going to school every day, doing homework, and keeping up with your extracurricular activities, you should have a substantial amount of extra time this summer. Do the Freakish thing, and *don't* waste it!

Spend more time networking, reading, watching YouTube videos (those that teach you something), listening to podcasts, and anything else that furthers your mission of early FI. Not being a full-time student (even if just for a couple of months) is an opportunity to spend even more time supercharging your journey to early FI.

Also, keep an eye on that post–high school budget you built in the last Phase. You'll need to make some adjustments, but try to stick to what you envisioned to maximize your savings rate.

College-Bound Freaks

If you are headed to college this fall, this summer is just a short break from your studies. But that doesn't mean you can't maximize its potential. Spend some of your extra time earning and saving (Mechanisms 1 and 3). Your additional income may come from a full-time job, a part-time job, your current side hustle(s), a new side hustle, a passive income stream, or a combination of these. Keep in mind the income requirements needed to qualify for a future mortgage if you plan to buy your first real estate property in the next few years.

Also consider taking a college course or two to get a head start on your certificate or degree. If you are close to the school you'll be attending, take a couple of courses on campus. You could also look into online class offerings or take a couple of classes at a local community college that will transfer to your college of choice. If you can rack up enough early college credits, you may be able to graduate or finish your program early and save thousands of dollars.

Non-College-Bound Freaks

It's time to enter the real world and get a full-time job. Whether you'll be living at home, renting a room in someone else's house hack, or making some other living arrangement, you need to start earning that dough! Earn money from more than one revenue stream (Mechanism 1), keep your expenses low (Mechanism 2), crush your savings rate (Mechanism 3), and begin to hammer your investments (Mechanism 4). You should be in full-on FI Freak mode!

Talk to Your Parent(s) About Health Insurance

You need health insurance. Period. In high school, you were probably on a parent's health insurance plan. Staying there is typically the best option until you either get your own healthcare coverage through an employer or are too old to stay on their plan.

Generally, you can stay on a parent's plan until you are 26. But laws change, and things can vary from state to state. You may need to do a little investigating to see what's best for you and your family. Discuss the following options with your parents:

- Staying on their plan (maybe you pay for your share?)
- Starting your own individual health insurance plan (since you are young and healthy, it may be less expensive than staying on your parent's plan)
- Enrolling in the student health plan at your college or university
- Enrolling in your employer's plan

Go to biggerpockets.com/teenworkbook for a couple of resources to get you started.

I WILL GET MY HEALTH INSURANCE THROUGH:

If You Are Going to College, Choose Your Major Wisely

If you are continuing your education, you need to decide what course of study you'll pursue. I give some tips on picking a promising major in Chapter Twenty-Seven of *First to a Million*. Go back to that chapter, find the section titled "Pick a Promising Major," and review my advice. Also, go back to Freak Phase 5 and look at your notes under the task "Start Narrowing Down Possible Career Paths or Jobs."

Try to pick a major that will lead to a career that is in high demand and has a high opportunity level. If REI has piqued your interest, consider a school where you can study real estate.

MY COLLEGE MAJOR WILL BE:

Manage Your Expenses After High School

Our culture says your smart phone is no longer good enough six months after you purchased it. That you must drive the best cars you can afford, live in the best house you can afford, stay in the best hotels you can afford, and live the best life you can afford.

—BRANDON TURNER, "HOW TO BECOME A MILLIONAIRE," WWW.BIGGERPOCKETS.COM

Things are different now, no matter what your post–high school plans may be. It's time to take control of your personal finances and manage them like the FI Freak you are. In the last Phase, you created a projected budget for your life after high school, which is a great start. But let's dig a little deeper and make sure you're on track and maximizing Mechanism 2.

Food

In Chapter Eighteen in *First to a Million*, I go over strategies to save money on food. There are also some beneficial resources for that chapter in Appendix B, which are also linked at biggerpockets. com/teenworkbook. Review all this information to make sure you are being frugal with your food spending. Remember, food is the third-largest expense for Americans.

Transportation

I will again refer you to Chapter Eighteen in *First to a Million* to review strategies for saving on the second-largest expense for Americans: transportation. If you are moving out of your family's home, you can be strategic about where you live next to save money on this expense.

Do what you can to live close to your school or workplace. The closer you are, the less need you have for a car. If you can get rid of your car (assuming you have one now), you'll reduce your transportation expenses significantly as your gas, insurance, depreciation, maintenance, parking, and repair costs magically disappear. Strongly consider walking, biking, carpooling, and using public transportation and rideshares as alternatives that can save you thousands of dollars every year.

Avoid Lifestyle Inflation

This message is for all you FI Freaks. If you are entering the workforce full-time, you need to hear this now. If you are headed to college, this message is essential for when you finish school and get a full-time job with your certificate or degree.

FREAK SPEAK

FS

LIFESTYLE INFLATION: The tendency to increase your spending as you make more money.

When you start making more money, it is much harder than you might think to *not* increase your spending. This is especially true when your friends are increasing their spending and giving you grief about why you aren't doing the same.

Be vigilant about keeping your spending habits consistent over time and keeping them low. You won't need to do that forever—just until you reach FI. At that point, you can reevaluate your spending and increase in some of the areas you value most. If you can keep your spending low from now until FI, it will pay you back richly and supercharge your journey to FI.

I love this anecdote from Chad Carson's book *Retire Early with Real Estate* regarding lifestyle inflation. It's about a young person named Louis who is seeking advice from a mentor. One day, the old man asked him, "Louis, do you want to know how to become rich?"

"Of course!" Louis enthusiastically responded.

"If you want to be rich, you need to learn to live on less than you earn. If you earn $40,000, live on less than $40,000. Got it, Louis?"

"Got it!"

"Next, you need to earn $80,000. But you need to still live on $40,000. Got it, Louis?"

"Got it!"

"Finally, you need to earn $120,000. But you need to still live on $40,000. Got it, Louis?"

"Yes, got it!"

"Louis, if you keep doing that, you can't help but become rich. And it will happen faster than you think."

List some ways you'll keep your housing, transportation, food, and other costs low:

1. _____

2. _____

3. _____

4. _____

5. _____

6. _____

7. _____

8. _____

9. _____

10. _____

Start Another Passive Income Stream

To level up Mechanism 1, you started your first passive income stream in Freak Phase 4. Hopefully, that is going well and you're seeing the power of passive income for your financial future. The passive income stream you started back then was probably a simple one.

Whatever stream you started then, this is a perfect time to reevaluate its success. Ask yourself these questions to make some decisions around the future of that endeavor:

Q. How much income has this passive income stream provided?

A.

Q. Are there indications it will grow in the future? If so, what are they?

A.

Q. What time, effort, or money could I invest in taking this to the next level?

A.

Q. What changes can I make to my stream that might make it more successful?

A.

After serious reflection on those questions, you need to decide what to do with the existing passive income stream. You could:

1. Keep it as is.
2. Improve it.
3. Let it go.

Once you've decided what to do with your current passive income stream, create a plan to execute it. **Write your list of action steps here:**

ACTION STEPS
FOR THIS FREAK PHASE

1.

2.

3.

4.

5.

Regardless of what you decide to do with your first passive income stream, it's time to start building another. This summer is the perfect time to start researching, creating, and implementing another passive income stream that will help fuel your early FI efforts.

Here is the same list of possibilities from Freak Phase 4. See if one of them sounds more interesting to you now. If not, simply google "passive income ideas" and find something that will work for you.

- Buying rental properties
- Owning vending machines
- Owning self-serve car washes
- Owning laundromats
- Owning self-storage rentals
- Selling an e-book you've written
- Selling stock photos you've taken
- Selling an online course you've created
- Investing in dividend stocks
- Investing in real estate investment trusts (REITs)
- Putting money in high-yield savings accounts
- Renting out your garage
- Getting paid to put an ad on your car
- Renting out your car on Turo

Once you pick a new passive income stream, research it online and write down in the space below the key information you find. Most important, put together a timeline of tasks and due dates to get your new passive income stream up and running.

INFORMATION FOR MY NEW PASSIVE INCOME STREAM

DUE DATES	✓	TASK TO COMPLETE
	◯	
	◯	
	◯	
	◯	
	◯	
	◯	
	◯	
	◯	

✚ Put any needed **REMINDERS** in your calendar.

Continue Investing in Index Funds

In the previous two tasks, we focused on minimizing your expenses and building your passive income. Here we will revisit your contributions to index funds, which are increasing your ability to have future sustainable asset withdrawal. With these three tasks, you are strengthening your position to satisfy the FI equation:

$$Passive\ Income + Sustainable\ Asset\ Withdrawals > Living\ expenses$$

This task is just about checking in on your index fund investing strategy and your progress with Mechanism 4. At this point, you should have accomplished the following:

- Created a future investment savings account
- Established a system for depositing money into this account, provided your emergency fund is fully funded
- Decided on your investing ratio
- Opened a brokerage account
- Established a system for transferring money from your future investment savings account into your brokerage account
- Established a system for investing cash in your brokerage account in an index fund

Reevaluate the systems you have in place for investing in index funds. Make any necessary adjustments or improvements. If you have been doing your transactions manually on your phone's apps but now have a steady monthly income, set up auto transfers. (See the "Open a Brokerage Account" task in Freak Phase 4.5 for detailed instructions.)

Watch the Documentary *Playing with Fire*

This 2019 documentary is about 90 minutes long and highlights one couple's transition from the traditional American Dream pathway to a FIRE mindset.

The documentary's website says:

> *Playing with FIRE follows 35-year-old Scott Rieckens, his wife Taylor, and their toddler Jovie as they embark on a year-long odyssey to understand the rules of this [FIRE] sub-culture and test their willingness to reject the standard narrative of adult life, which basically prescribes: "Go to college, take out tons of student loans, buy a new car, take on a mortgage, buy another car and lots more stuff you don't need, then work for 40+ years to pay for it all. If you're lucky, you might be able to retire at 65 and not have to live on beans."*

You'll likely have to pay to watch the film, but it's worth every penny. A link to the documentary can be found at biggerpockets.com/teenworkbook.

List your five main takeaways from the documentary here:

Continue to Learn About Real Estate Investing

In Chapter Twenty-Five of *First to a Million*, I introduce the concept of leverage as it applies to REI, including its pros and cons. You should review both sections about leverage in Chapter Twenty-Five as a refresher before moving on.

 LEVERAGE: The use of borrowed money to increase the potential return of an investment. The goal is to earn a return greater than the interest you paid to borrow the money.

Using leverage in real estate can help you achieve a much larger return on your investment. Let's look at an example, assuming you have $2,000 to invest. You are going to invest $1,000 in a company's stock and $1,000 in real estate.

If you invested $1,000 in a company's stock, then you own $1,000 of stock. That $1,000 of stock is working to make you more money. You have zero leverage.

Now let's say you invest the other $1,000 in real estate. (You can't buy much real estate with $1,000, but to keep things simple, assume you can.) You decide to buy a condo as an investment. If you found a condo for sale for $1,000, you could buy it with the $1,000 you have. You wouldn't need to borrow any money. As with your stock investment, you would have zero leverage.

But you could also buy a condo worth $4,000 (an improbably good price for a condo, but let's go with it for the sake of example). In this case, let's say you obtained a mortgage (loan) from a bank to buy the condo. You would pay your $1,000 in cash and get a mortgage for the remaining $3,000 needed for the purchase. The bank lending you the $3,000 won't let you use their money for free. They will charge you interest, but the interest charges are built into and accounted for in your monthly cash flow figures. You now have $4,000 working for you! You have leveraged your $1,000 into $4,000.

Here's where leverage gets interesting. Assume that both the stock and the condo earn a return of 10 percent. Let's look at what these two investments have done for you after one year.

Stock Investment

This one is easy. You invested $1,000, and it had a return of 10 percent. You now have $1,100. You've made $100.

Real Estate Investment

This one is a little different. To keep things simple, let's assume the condo's 10 percent return is a combination of all four ways that real estate builds wealth: cash flow, appreciation, loan paydown, and tax benefits. (See the beginning of Chapter Twenty-Five in *First to a Million*.) The condo's initial value was $4,000. It had a return of 10 percent. You've made $400.

Without leverage, you took $1,000 and turned it into $1,100.

With leverage, you took $1,000 and turned it into $1,400. That's $300 more.

Does $300 seem like a lot of money? Maybe, maybe not. But what if you had $100,000 to invest, not just $1,000? If that were the case, would an extra $30,000 make you smile? I'm guessing it would!

The downside

In the examples above, we said that both investments earned a 10 percent return. What if things went wrong and they both had a return of negative 10 percent? (It can happen—*all* investments involve risk.) If so, you would lose less money with the stock investment than with the condo investment. Leverage multiplies your return, whether it's positive or negative. So, what should you do?

If I thought that keeping your money safe by not investing it or that investing only in unleveraged options to minimize losses were the best options for you, I would say so. If you follow the *First to a Million* workbook, you'll make intelligent and strategic REI decisions. This will decrease your risk of losing money and increase your risk of building wealth. To reach early FI, you must take calculated risks. That's the Freakish truth.

Congratulations!

You've just completed Freak Phase 7! It's time to be proud of your Freakishness and check in with your progress. Post a video of yourself describing the three most meaningful tasks you completed in this Freak Phase, and post a picture of yourself with your completed checklist from the beginning of this Phase.

Don't forget to use **#FREAKPHASE7** and **#TEENAGEFIFREAK** and to tag **@SHEEKSFREAKS** and **@BIGGERPOCKETS!**

Now
Go Out
There And
Get Your
Freak On!

FREAK PHASE Eight

SEPTEMBER–DECEMBER
(If in college, first semester of freshman year)

Some of the smartest people I know are some of the people who struggle with their finances the most because they outsmart themselves. It's like they look into it too much, and they find a reason why it might not work after looking at 500 reasons why it could work. The difference is ... once you identify an opportunity that is profitable ... don't ask any more questions ... What are you waiting for?

—SCOTT MCGILLIVRAY ON *THE BIGGERPOCKETS PODCAST*, EPISODE 434

Here is the checklist for this four-month Freak Phase. It's best to read the entire Freak Phase before filling in the due date for each item. Don't forget to use your calendar to help you stay on track. And remember—you're a FI Freak, so you've got this!

DUE DATES	✓	TASK
	◯	Read *The Simple Path to Wealth* by JL Collins.
	◯	Create a new social environment.
	◯	Reevaluate your emergency fund.
	◯	Do a status check on your other savings accounts.
	◯	Find a job while in college.
	◯	Start analyzing properties.
	◯	Set three financial goals.
	◯	Implement a new Freak Tweak.
	◯	Sell a personal item you no longer need or want.
	◯	Find and do a new fun, free activity.
	◯	Interview someone who is where you want to be.
	◯	Evaluate your income streams.
	◯	Calculate and track your net worth.
	◯	Continue networking.
	◯	Shadow someone for a day.

+ACTION STEPS

DATE: _____

The date I communicated my three goals to my accountability partner.

Write out your three goals for this Freak Phase here.

1 ....

2 ....

3 ....

MY NEW "PAY YOURSELF FIRST"
PERCENTAGE GOAL IS: %

MY NEW
SAVINGS RATE GOAL IS: %

MONTH 1 / DATE COMPLETED

....

PERSON TO INTERVIEW

....

MONTH 2 / DATE COMPLETED

....

PERSON TO INTERVIEW

....

MONTH 3 / DATE COMPLETED

....

PERSON TO INTERVIEW

....

MONTH 4 / DATE COMPLETED

....

PERSON TO INTERVIEW

....

FOR FRUGALITY IS...

✛ Put a **RECURRING REMINDER** in your calendar to complete these tasks at the beginning of every Freak Phase.

Read *The Simple Path to Wealth* by JL Collins

Author and blogger JL Collins is one of the most well-known figures in the FIRE movement, and it's largely because of this fantastic book. *The Simple Path to Wealth* is about investing in the stock market to reach early FI. The idea behind it is that investing in the stock market does not need to be complicated or confusing. Collins discusses savings rates, index fund investing, why you should avoid bad debt, and other essential topics. Enjoy this one and take notes!

Create a New Social Environment

Surround yourself with only people who are going to lift you higher.

—OPRAH WINFREY

During this Phase, many of you will be relocating to attend college. Those of you who choose a different path may also be making a physical move to a new city or even a new state. No matter what your plans are, one thing is for sure: None of you will be spending as much time with your high school circle of friends as you used to. It's time to form a new circle, and you must do it correctly.

Back in Phase 2, you evaluated your core circle. Your core circle contains the four or five people you interact with the most. These are the people who have the greatest influence on how you spend your time each and every day. Take some time to be intentional about how you reform your core circle for your future. Ask yourself these questions:

1. What activities would I like to do most often with my core circle?
2. What topics and ideas would I love to discuss with my core circle?
3. How should the time I spend with my core circle advance my goals?
4. How should my core circle help make me a better person?
5. Do I want my core circle to challenge and inspire me?

You should also think beyond your core circle. What about clubs and organizations? If you are entering college, there will be many groups and clubs for you to join. From sororities and fraternities to social groups, academic groups, intramural sports teams, service-based organizations, and more, you'll have plenty of new groups to choose from.

If you are not attending college, you'll have many options in the professional world as well. You could join your local Real Estate Investors Association (REIA), local Meetup.com groups, or another adult group that will help you reach your goals. These groups could be in person, online, or both. You should also spend more time connecting and mingling inside of the BiggerPockets and SheeksFreaks communities.

The main point is this: Now that you're on an established path to early FI and you are a high school graduate, it's time to rethink who you choose to spend your time with. The people around you have an enormous impact on where you're headed and what you'll accomplish.

Choose who you hang out with wisely. Don't spend your time with late-night partiers, naysayers, and others who don't share your motivations and aspirations. Instead, be intentional about choosing friends, groups, and networks that align with your visions and values. Remember, simple minds discuss other people, average minds discuss events, and enlightened (Freakish) minds discuss ideas. You are *absolutely* in this latter group. To maximize your success, you need to find others like you.

Write out a vision for your core circle and social groups.

Write out your answers to the 5 questions listed earlier about your core circle

1 ....

2 ....

3 ....

4 ....

5 ....

| WHAT ARE SOME QUALITIES AND VALUES I WOULD LIKE THOSE IN MY CORE CIRCLE TO HAVE? | WHAT GROUPS, CLUBS, AND ORGANIZATIONS WOULD BE A GOOD FIT FOR MY GOALS AND ASPIRATIONS? |

+ Put any **REMINDERS** in your calendar that will assist you in joining these groups.

Reevaluate Your Emergency Fund

You know your emergency fund savings account should have enough cash to cover six months' worth of expenses. Now that your living situation and monthly expenses are changing, you need to reevaluate how much should be in your emergency fund. Depending on your situation, it may be best to wait until the end of this Phase. For example, if you have just started college, you'll be able to calculate your average monthly expenses more accurately after a few months of being there.

Others who are not attending college but have moved out of their family's home could be ready to recalculate their average expenses earlier in this Phase. Decide when would be the best time for you to do your recalculation, and set your due date accordingly.

When you are ready, you'll analyze your most recent months' expenses in your tracking app. Average your expenses over the last few months. Take the new total expense number and multiply it by six. Compare that with your current emergency fund.

If you need to add to your emergency fund, you might transfer the entire amount from your future investment savings account all at once. Or you could decide to add a few hundred dollars to the emergency fund every month until it is fully funded again.

$$\text{MY NEW AVERAGE MONTHLY EXPENSES} \quad \boxed{\text{x6} =} \quad \text{NEW EMERGENCY FUND AMOUNT}$$

Do a Status Check on Your Other Savings Accounts

This is also a great time to check the status of your future investment and "fun" fund savings accounts to make sure you are crushing Mechanism 3 like a true FI Freak. Hopefully, you have been contributing some money to both these accounts over the last couple of years. Ideally, you have also been using some money from your future investment account to invest in index funds. If you haven't been doing these things, don't fret. You'll get there. Checking in on your systems now will help you do that.

At this point, you want to be seeing these two accounts grow. If you are a full-time student, this will be more challenging than for someone who is working full-time, but do the best you can. If your goal is to buy your first house hack property in Phase 12, as this workbook advises, the future investment account should be looking pretty healthy. (In the next Phase, we'll take a detailed look at exactly how much you'll need to have saved to buy that first property.)

And what about your "fun" fund? Hopefully, you are using this to save for future sizable purchases that add joy and happiness to your life. One way to contribute to this account is to transfer a set amount from your checking account into your "fun" fund each month. Another way is to simply put any extra money left over from your budget each month in this account. Figure out what works best for you. Remember that your FI journey is not about sacrifice or withholding pleasure to the point of being unhappy. You should be enjoying the journey! If you aren't, you are not doing it correctly.

One last reminder: The money invested in index funds through your brokerage account is for the long term only—a *minimum* of ten years. Your index fund investments are *not* meant to be "holding" accounts where you keep your money until you need it elsewhere—say, for a down payment on a house hack property. If you plan on using a chunk of money in the next ten years, you should *not* invest it in the stock market.

What are the current balances in each of your accounts?

$0.⁰⁰	✓	ACCOUNT
	○	Checking Account
	○	Emergency Fund Savings Account
	○	Future Investment Savings Account
	○	"Fun" Fund Savings Account
	○	Brokerage Account (Cash)
	○	Index Fund Investments

✚ Put a **RECURRING REMINDER** in your calendar to check these balances every Phase.

Find a Job While in College

Don't forget about Mechanism 1 if you are now (or will soon be) attending college classes. It's time to start looking for a beneficial part-time job. Many opportunities will work well with your FI Freak goals, but remember that only W-2 jobs will be counted as income when you apply for your first mortgage.

In Chapter Sixteen of *First to a Million,* there was a short subsection called "Jobs While in College." I suggest you do a quick review of that section for a few great ideas to get you thinking about possible part-time jobs. If your side hustle or passive income efforts are finding success, don't stop them now! Think of ways you might grow that success while in school. Alternatively, go back to Phase 2 and look over the "Start a Side Hustle" task, or to Phase 4 and look over "Start a Passive Income Stream" to revisit ideas that may work better now that you're in college.

You should also continue to apply for scholarships. Just because you've begun college doesn't mean you can't continue to win additional money to help pay your bills. And make sure you stop by the student aid office on campus at least once every other week to nicely ask if there are any scholarships or new grants you can apply for. They will eventually get to know you and think of you first when some additional money does come in. Maybe bring the secretary a muffin to show your appreciation!

List some possible part-time jobs below:

POSITION_____

BUSINESS _____

CONTACT INFO_____

RATE OF PAY_____ DATE I APPLIED _____

OTHER NOTES_____

POSITION_____

BUSINESS _____

CONTACT INFO_____

RATE OF PAY_____ DATE I APPLIED _____

OTHER NOTES_____

POSITION_____

BUSINESS _____

CONTACT INFO_____

RATE OF PAY_____ DATE I APPLIED _____

OTHER NOTES_____

POSITION_____

BUSINESS _____

CONTACT INFO_____

RATE OF PAY_____ DATE I APPLIED _____

OTHER NOTES_____

✛ Put a **RECURRING REMINDER** in your calendar to stop by your school's financial aid office every two weeks to check on available scholarships, grants, and other monies.

Start Analyzing Properties

You have now read two books with detailed instructions on analyzing potential REI properties. In *The House Hacking Strategy*, Craig Curelop discusses this skill in Chapter Seven. Brandon Turner goes over more property-analyzing strategies in Chapter Five of *The Book on Rental Property Investing*. You should review both those chapters now.

FREAK TECHNIQUE

ANALYZING PROPERTIES: Evaluating the numbers on a potential investment property to determine if a property meets your specific metrics.

To analyze properties accurately, you should first determine the area where you want to buy. If you are on pace to buy your first property toward the end of Phase 12, ask yourself where you'll want to live at that time. (If you're not sure where you'll be living yet, that's okay. We'll tackle that decision in Phase 10.) You don't need to narrow it down to the exact neighborhood. Try limiting the area to within a twenty-mile radius of where you see yourself living. A twenty-mile radius is pretty big, but it gives you a much higher chance of finding a good deal for your first purchase!

Next, get to know the different neighborhoods within that radius by driving and walking around the area. The more familiar you are with these neighborhoods, the better you'll be able to determine if a property's listing price is high or low. Visit biggerpockets.com/teenworkbook for a link to a great YouTube video showing you how to analyze properties.

There are several property analysis calculators out there. BiggerPockets has some great ones that you can use a few times for free. I also have a free, simple one you can use. For links to these calculators, go to biggerpockets.com/teenworkbook.

✛ Put a **RECURRING REMINDER** in your calendar to analyze five properties per week. Use the log on the next page to keep track of the properties you analyze. Feel free to modify it for your specific criteria and market.

Use this log for your first week of property analysis—after that, start a spreadsheet using these criteria (and anything else you find important) to track the properties you analyze. With five properties a week, the numbers will start adding up quick!

WEEKLY PROPERTY ANALYSIS LOG

PROPERTY ADDRESS		
NO. OF BEDS & BATHS		
SINGLE FAMILY OR MULTIFAMILY		
LIST PRICE		
PRICE PER SQUARE FOOT		
REHAB NEEDED?		
ESTIMATED MONTHLY RENTAL INCOME		
OTHER NOTES		

Congratulations!

You've just completed
Freak Phase 8! It's time to be proud of your
Freakishness and check in with your progress.
Post a video of yourself describing the three
most meaningful tasks you completed in this
Freak Phase, and post a picture of yourself
with your completed checklist from the
beginning of this Phase.

Don't forget to use **#FREAKPHASE8**
and **#TEENAGEFIFREAK** and to tag
@SHEEKSFREAKS and **@BIGGERPOCKETS!**

Now go out there
and get your freak on!

FREAK PHASE *Nine*

JANUARY–APRIL
(If in college, second semester of freshman year)

If the concept of early financial freedom strikes a chord, if you are convinced this should be your goal, then you'll experience a powerful emotional urge to pursue this goal. Early financial freedom should be a powerful motivator. The result of attaining financial freedom is a life lived on your terms.

—SCOTT TRENCH, *SET FOR LIFE*

Here is the checklist for this four-month Freak Phase. It's best to read the entire Freak Phase before filling in the due date for each item. Don't forget to use your calendar to help you stay on track. And remember—you're a FI Freak, so you've got this!

DUE DATES	✓	TASK
	○	Read *The Book on Managing Rental Properties* by Heather and Brandon Turner.
	○	Read *First-Time Home Buyer* by Scott Trench and Mindy Jensen.
	○	Start to check your credit scores regularly.
	○	Take your networking efforts to the next level.
	○	Evaluate your income streams.
	○	Set three financial goals.
	○	Implement a new Freak Tweak.
	○	Sell a personal item you no longer need or want.
	○	Find and do a new fun, free activity.
	○	Interview someone who is where you want to be.
	○	Calculate and track your net worth.
	○	Shadow someone for a day.

DATE: _____

The date I communicated my three goals to my accountability partner.

Write out your three goals for this Freak Phase here.

1 ....

2 ....

3 ....

MY NEW "PAY YOURSELF FIRST"
PERCENTAGE
GOAL IS: %

MY NEW
SAVINGS RATE
GOAL IS: %

INTERVIEW Log

FREAK Tweak
FOR FRUGALITY IS...

MONTH 1 / DATE COMPLETED

....

PERSON TO INTERVIEW

MONTH 2 / DATE COMPLETED

....

PERSON TO INTERVIEW

MONTH 3 / DATE COMPLETED

....

PERSON TO INTERVIEW

MONTH 4 / DATE COMPLETED

....

PERSON TO INTERVIEW

....

Put a **RECURRING REMINDER** in your calendar to complete these tasks at the beginning of every Freak Phase.

Read *The Book on Managing Rental Properties* by Heather and Brandon Turner

Whether you're one year away from buying your first real estate property or five years away, this book will lay the foundation for your management systems and strategies. Take copious notes or do lots of highlighting. This information will be invaluable when the time comes.

Read *First-Time Home Buyer* by Scott Trench and Mindy Jensen

Since this workbook has many of you on track to buy your first property in a little over a year, this book is critical. It covers *all* the important aspects of buying that first property and doing it successfully. Once you've read this book as well, you can rest assured you have the fundamental knowledge down.

Start to Check Your Credit Scores Regularly

Building an excellent credit score is vital in your journey to early FI. At this point, you've been working on it for at least a few months by making on-time monthly payments on your credit card. On your 19th birthday, you should apply for your second credit card, and at 19½ you should apply for your third. (You should have already set calendar reminders to do so.) By using credit cards responsibly, you'll successfully build your credit history and score.

For a refresher on credit scores, you can reread Chapter Eleven of *First to a Million* and read the blog post linked at biggerpockets.com/teenworkbook.

It's now time to start checking your credit history and credit score. You'll have to do this regularly for two reasons:

1. To verify your credit score is improving.
2. To make sure the information on your credit reports is accurate.

FREAK TECHNIQUE

PERIODICALLY CHECKING CREDIT SCORES AND REPORTS: A scheduled process for verifying that your credit score is excellent and your credit reports are accurate.

Checking Your Credit Reports

The website you'll use to check your credit reports is www.annualcreditreport.com. This is the *only* website you should use, because it allows you to access your credit report at all three credit bureaus. The law allows you to check your credit report for free once a year at each of the three bureaus. I recommend spreading these out.

- On March 1st of each year, visit www.annualcreditreport.com. Request your **Experian** credit report. Look over the entire report to make sure there are no errors.
- On July 1st of each year, visit www.annualcreditreport.com. Request your **TransUnion** credit report. Look over the entire report to make sure there are no errors.
- On November 1st of each year, visit www.annualcreditreport.com. Request your **Equifax** credit report. Look over the entire report to make sure there are no errors.

Feel free to adjust this schedule as needed. By checking one of your credit reports every four months, you increase the likelihood of finding errors quickly. Although this process allows you to see your credit *reports*, it will not allow you to see your credit *scores*.

✚ Put a **RECURRING REMINDER** in your calendar to check one credit report every four months, as suggested above.

Checking Your Credit Scores

You should also check your credit scores. There are a few websites that let you do this for free. But be careful, as many websites will make it *seem* like their services are free, when they're actually not. I recommend www.creditkarma.com. Once you create an account with one of these sites, they will let you see your credit scores for one or more of the three credit bureaus, and you can check back often. They will also send you updates (emails or texts) if your score changes or something looks suspicious. They do this for free because they hope you'll purchase one of the many services offered on their website. Just an FYI: You don't need those extra services.

✚ Put a **RECURRING REMINDER** in your calendar to check your credit scores at least every other month.

Use a chart like this to track your credit scores over time:

DATE	EQUIFAX	experian	TransUnion

Another Suggestion

If you are having trouble building your credit score, here's an option to consider: Talk to your local bank (perhaps the bank where you have your checking account) about getting a personal loan. If they give you a personal loan, it will likely be for a low amount, such as $500. That is okay.

The strategy is to take out the loan *only* for the opportunity to make on-time monthly payments, which will help boost your credit score. Do not spend the $500—just make the monthly loan payments on time *with* the money you borrowed. You'll be charged some interest, but it's a small price to pay to boost your credit score!

Take Your Networking Efforts to the Next Level

It's time to review your networking efforts again. Networking is one of the most crucial aspects of your early FI journey. Do not take it lightly! The more people in your network, the easier your path to early FI will be.

In Phase 2, you started your networking endeavors, and in Phases 3 and 4, you leveled them up a notch. Now it's time to supercharge them!

In Phase 3, you started a Google Sheet (or something similar) to keep track of all your contacts. How's that looking? Is it updated and current? Are you adding new people regularly? Are you touching base with everyone on your list at least once a Phase? If your list has become too long, you can prioritize it and reach out more often to the people who are most valuable to your future goals.

As a reminder, your list should include:

- Their name
- Their contact info (phone number, email address, or account profile)
- What they do
- Where they live (including their time zone)
- What you've talked about
- Where you met them
- The last time you interacted with them
- Any other relevant information

Are you using your accounts on LinkedIn, BiggerPockets, and SheeksFreaks to their full networking potential? These are the best communities for finding people to build your network. But remember, simply following or connecting with them on the platform is not enough. You need to have conversations with people. Maximize your networking returns with phone calls, Zoom meetings, FaceTime chats, emails, DMs, or messages sent through LinkedIn, BiggerPockets, and SheeksFreaks.

Although these strategies are effective, they don't compare to an in-person conversation. The most significant networking returns happen when you talk to face-to-face. Take someone out to lunch or for coffee.

You could also go to a meetup. Attend a BiggerPockets event in your area or register for a conference or seminar, and talk to people at these events. You don't have to talk to everyone. Instead, set a goal of having a meaningful conversation with four people. Each conversation should last *at least* fifteen minutes. During that time, ask them plenty of questions about what they're up to and what projects they are currently working on. See if there is a way you could help *them* reach their goals. And don't forget to ask for their contact information so you can add them to your networking list!

✦✦ Put any needed **REMINDERS (RECURRING OR ONE-TIME)** in your calendar.

Write down some actions, events, or strategies you'll complete during each month of this Phase to expand your network.

MONTH 1

MONTH 2

MONTH 3

Evaluate Your Income Streams

You should have a recurring reminder in your calendar to complete this task every Phase, but it is so important that I want to make sure you complete it again now! As we go through life, we get caught up in the hustle and bustle of day-to-day living, and it's challenging to take a step back and look at the big picture. But taking that step back is vital to make sure you are maximizing your returns and not missing any opportunities.

Complete this task to see if you should make any changes to your revenue-generating efforts as you hammer Mechanism 1. When evaluating them, zoom out and analyze your efforts from a high level—look at them from a long-term strategic viewpoint.

Ask yourself these questions and contemplate the answers:

- How is my part-time or full-time job going?
  - What benefits am I getting from this job other than a paycheck?
  - Does the job have a flexible schedule?
  - Am I able to work on other projects that help me reach my goals while on the clock?
  - Do my coworkers or boss inspire me?
  - Am I learning while I'm earning?
  - Is the job giving me verifiable W-2 income to help with a future mortgage approval?
  - Is the commute short, helping me keep my transportation expenses low?
- How is my side hustle(s) going?
  - How much am I making per hour?
  - Is this endeavor opening other doors for me?
  - Are there indications it will see larger returns in the future?
  - Do I enjoy my time spent on this side hustle?
  - Do I need to hire some help for this side hustle to grow?
  - What else needs to happen for my side hustle to grow and prosper? What resources could I use? Who might I talk to for advice?
  - Am I keeping track of my earnings from my side hustle when I track my income and expenses? (Knowing your total revenue is helpful when periodically evaluating a side hustle.)
  - If I discontinue this side hustle, what other options exist for me now?

- How are my passive income streams doing?
  - How much time do I spend on these? (Passive income is rarely 100 percent passive.)
  - How much am I making per hour on each passive income stream?
  - Are there indications these will grow in the future?
  - Should I invest more money or time in one of my passive income streams?
  - Are there other passive income opportunities I should explore?
  - What else needs to happen for my passive income streams to grow and prosper? What resources could I use? Who might I talk to for advice?
  - Am I keeping track of my earnings from my passive income streams when I track my income and expenses?

Based on the answers to these questions, what steps should you take during this Phase to improve your income-generating efforts?

✚ Put any needed REMINDERS (RECURRING OR ONE-TIME) in your calendar.

INCOME-GENERATING ACTION STEPS
FOR THIS FREAK PHASE

1.

2.

3.

4.

5.

CONGRATULATIONS!

You've just completed Freak Phase 9! It's time to be proud of your Freakishness and check in with your progress. Post a video of yourself describing the three most meaningful tasks you completed in this Freak Phase, and post a picture of yourself with your completed checklist from the beginning of this Phase.

Don't forget to use **#FREAKPHASE9** and **#TEENAGEFIFREAK** and to tag **@SHEEKSFREAKS** and **@BIGGERPOCKETS!**

NOW GO OUT THERE AND GET YOUR FREAK ON!

FREAK PHASE
Ten

MAY–AUGUST
(If in college, summer after freshman year)

There is no passion to be found playing small—in settling for a life that's less than the one you are capable of living.

—NELSON MANDELA

Here is the checklist for this four-month Freak Phase. It's best to read the entire Freak Phase before filling in the due date for each item. Don't forget to use your calendar to help you stay on track. And remember—you're a FI Freak, so you've got this!

DUE DATES	✓	TASK
	○	Read *Think and Grow Rich* by Napoleon Hill.
	○	Decide on the market area for your first real estate purchase.
	○	Determine how much money you'll need to buy your first property.
	○	Reevaluate your investing ratio.
	○	Reevaluate how well you are paying yourself first.
	○	Set three financial goals.
	○	Implement a new Freak Tweak.
	○	Sell a personal item you no longer need or want.
	○	Find and do a new fun, free activity.
	○	Interview someone who is where you want to be.
	○	Evaluate your income streams.
	○	Calculate and track your net worth.
	○	Continue networking.
	○	Shadow someone for a day.

Goals
+ACTION STEPS

The date I communicated my three goals to my accountability partner.

Write out your three goals for this Freak Phase here.

1 ....

2 ....

3 ....

MY NEW "PAY YOURSELF FIRST"
PERCENTAGE
GOAL IS: %

MY NEW
SAVINGS RATE
GOAL IS: %

FOR FRUGALITY IS...

MONTH 1 / DATE COMPLETED

....

PERSON TO INTERVIEW

....

MONTH 2 / DATE COMPLETED

....

PERSON TO INTERVIEW

....

MONTH 3 / DATE COMPLETED

....

PERSON TO INTERVIEW

....

MONTH 4 / DATE COMPLETED

....

PERSON TO INTERVIEW

....

Put a **RECURRING REMINDER** in your calendar to complete these tasks at the beginning of every Freak Phase.

Read *Think and Grow Rich* by Napoleon Hill

The original version, published in 1937, was the first book to boldly ask, "What makes a winner?" The author developed the "Law of Success" philosophy that is the foundation for this book and others he wrote. It dives into the way we think, both consciously and subconsciously, and how that affects our behavior and our success. Enjoy. This one is life-changing! There are a few updated versions of this book available. I recommend the 2005 edition published by TarcherPerigee.

Decide on the Market Area for Your First Real Estate Purchase

Whether you are on track to buy your first REI property in Phase 12 (around April or May of next year) or soon after, let's take some time to decide where you'll be buying.

You have been introduced to several strategies, such as house hacking, the BRRRR method, fix and flip, live-in fix and flip, and out-of-state investing. Although all can be very successful, I recommend doing a house hack first because it is the best strategy by far for young first-time real estate investors.

Once you have a successful house hack or two under your belt, you'll have enough experience to venture into other strategies. For example, after you've managed minor upgrades, repairs, and maintenance on your house hack, you should be much more successful at managing a rehab project with a contractor on a BRRRR or live-in fix and flip.

If you decide to house hack your first purchase, choosing your market is much easier since you'll be living in the property you buy. Therefore, the obvious question is: Where will you be living next year?

To complete this task, you need to decide where you'll be living for the twelve months following the purchase of your first property. As I said at the end of Phase 8 when we examined the task of analyzing properties—you don't have to narrow down your market area to an exact neighborhood. Instead, try narrowing it down to a much larger twenty-mile radius of where you see yourself living. This generous target area gives you a much better chance of finding a good deal for your first purchase.

If you're in college, you may be thinking, "I'll be in my college town until I graduate, but then I plan on moving, so should I still get a house hack property in my college town?" Great question. And the answer is easy: Yes! Don't wait to buy your first property *only* because you'll be moving in a couple of years.

Note: If you know you'll be moving two years after you buy the property and are confident that your exit strategy will be to sell it at that time, then consider living in that one house hack for the entire two years. That way you won't have to pay any capital gains tax on the appreciation of the property when you sell it—which could result in massive savings. (We went over this strategy at the end of Phase 6, in the task "Continue to Learn About Real Estate Investing.") Of course, all markets are different, so talk to an expert in your local area to get more personalized advice.

Another thing to consider is proximity to your school or job. We have discussed the importance of living as close to your school or job as possible to significantly decrease your transportation expenses. However, it is more than okay to add or lengthen a commute to find the best possible property for your first house hack. The amount of wealth and experience you'll gain from acquiring and managing it will *far* outweigh any increase in transportation expenses. So don't eliminate areas and communities just to stay close to the neighborhood where you work or attend classes.

Determine How Much Money You'll Need to Buy Your First Property

This is critical. The value of your property will determine your down payment, which will account for the largest portion of the money you'll need to have saved. And since different markets can have significantly different property values, it's impossible to tell you *the* magic number. But we'll calculate it as best we can.

There are five financial components you'll need to account for with your first purchase. They are:

- Down payment
- Closing costs
- Initial repairs and upgrades
- Reserves
- Your next purchase

Down payment

Since your house hack property will be a primary residence, you'll be eligible to put down less than the industry standard of 20 percent of the purchase price. Depending on the loan you choose, your down payment could be as low as 3 percent. It could be even lower with first-time homebuyer incentives. (In the next Freak Phase, you'll begin talking to lenders for your first purchase. The workbook will remind you to ask those lenders about the best loan options for you, any current incentives for first-time homebuyers, and other opportunities.)

You want your down payment to be as small as possible. One reason is that the amount needed for the down payment could decide whether you can even buy your first property. If you don't have a lot of money saved for REI in your future investment fund, a small down payment may be the only way to make it happen. A small down payment also allows you to maximize your leverage and cash-on-cash return. A final benefit is that you are keeping more money for your next purchase down the road. (If you want to follow Craig Curelop's example from *The House Hacking Strategy*, the goal is to do one house hack every year for a few years.)

FREAK SPEAK

CASH-ON-CASH RETURN: The cash income earned on the cash invested in a property, expressed as a percentage (cash income earned divided by cash invested).

One drawback to a low down payment is that you are taking on more risk, since you have a smaller amount of equity in the property and a higher mortgage payment. But taking calculated risks is what FI Freaks do to reach early FI. If you are not comfortable with the amount of risk, you should wait until you have enough saved for a larger down payment.

Another disadvantage of a small down payment is that you'll have to pay PMI (private mortgage insurance) if you choose a conventional loan, or you'll have to pay a higher MIP (mortgage insurance premium) if you use an FHA loan. However, you will account for these additional costs when you analyze each property, so they are a built-in cost of investing.

 EQUITY: The total value you have in an investment. Equity equals the current value of an investment minus the amount you owe on that investment.

In Phase 8, you began regularly analyzing properties in your expected market. Now that you've been doing this for a few months, you should have an excellent idea of what your potential house hack property should cost. For now, let's assume your down payment will be 4 percent of the purchase price. Using these two numbers, you can calculate your expected down payment.

Closing Costs

Closing costs can vary quite a bit, and there are creative ways to "move" those costs into your mortgage. Many closing costs can also be assigned to the seller while negotiating the deal. That's why determining an exact number is very difficult.

There are online closing cost calculators you can use to help estimate this expense. Visit biggerpockets. com/teenworkbook for links to two of these calculators.

Initial Repairs And Upgrades

Almost every property needs some work when you first move in. The most common expenses are paint, carpet/flooring, and minor upgrades, such as light fixtures or a new kitchen sink. As I mentioned before, I suggest avoiding major rehab or renovation projects for your first property. However, getting your hands dirty (or hiring someone else to get their hands dirty) by completing some minor repairs, upgrades, or improvements is a great way to make your property more desirable to potential tenants.

When you analyze a property, you'll include the estimated amount needed to make the property rent-ready. This can vary quite a bit. To complete this task with the final amount needed to buy your first property, assume you'll have $10,000 in initial repairs and upgrades, but understand that this amount can vary quite a bit based on the condition of the property.

Reserves

You *always* want to have reserves! If the first three expenses we just discussed would drain your future investment fund, leaving you no money for reserves, then you are *not* ready to buy your first property. You need to save more money.

Things will always go wrong, break, or need repairs. *Always.* What if you have an unexpected vacancy? What if a water heater and a dishwasher both need to be replaced in the same month? What if a tenant causes damage beyond what their security deposit will cover? Think of your reserves as an emergency fund for your investment property. Just as in your personal life, unexpected things will happen that have to be taken care of right away.

VACANCY: A rental unit with no renter and, therefore, no rental income.

Phase 12 will instruct you to create new bank accounts for your first property. Doing this will make it easy to keep your property's money separate from your other accounts. You will move your property's reserve funds into one of these new accounts so that you don't spend them on something else. The property's reserves should only be used for unexpected costs.

The larger and more expensive your property, the more reserves you should have. I recommend between $10,000 and $15,000 in reserves per property. The amount you choose will depend on your risk tolerance—that is, your ability to sleep at night if you choose to take on greater risk by maintaining lower reserves.

Your Next Purchase

If you want to take the fast track to early FI, start thinking about your second real estate purchase now. Buying your first property will be a considerable accomplishment, but it will probably motivate you to buy your next one as soon as you can. As I mentioned before, buying one house hack property a year for a few years is an excellent way to build your wealth while also expediting your journey to FI.

For this reason, you should keep as much money as possible in your future investment fund earmarked for a future real estate purchase. This is important to make sure you are ready to go when the time comes to buy that second property.

Use this chart to see if you have enough saved to buy your first property.

Current amount in my future investment savings account earmarked for a real estate investment	$
Subtract amount needed for a down payment	– $
Subtract amount needed for closing costs	– $
Subtract amount needed for initial repairs and upgrades	– $
Subtract amount needed for reserves	– $
EQUALS	= $

If **negative,** this is how much I need to save to be ready to buy my first property

If **positive,** this is how much I will have left over to use for my second purchase

Reevaluate Your Investing Ratio

Now that you know how much you'll need to buy your first property, you may want to reevaluate your investing ratio to help you meet the goal of buying a property soon.

In Phase 4.5, you chose an investing ratio. This ratio was a percentage breakdown that determined how much of your saved money would go toward index fund investing and future real estate investing. Since you have been saving and investing for a while and are planning your first real estate purchase, now's the perfect time to review your investing ratio and tweak it if needed.

There is no correct answer here. It comes down to which investment strategy you prefer. You can always change whatever ratio you decide on whenever you want. Just the fact that you are young and are saving a large portion of your earnings to invest is pretty Freakish!

My new investing ratio is:

INDEX FUNDS	REAL ESTATE
%	%

Reevaluate How Well You Are Paying Yourself First

The last time we looked at how much you were paying yourself first was in Phase 6, when you analyzed your expenses after graduating from high school. It's time to look at this again while considering Mechanisms 1, 2, and 3.

You should be calculating your savings rate every month. Knowing your savings rate and tracking it over time are essential, but they're not quite the same as paying yourself first. To recap, paying yourself first is the percentage of your income you pay yourself every month *before* paying your other bills and expenses. Your savings rate, however, is how much you actually save each month. A savings rate can include additional money you had left after paying your bills and expenses, plus the money from when you paid yourself first.

Now that you have been consistently tracking your income and expenses, calculating your savings rate, and monitoring your various savings account levels, you can make an informed decision about how much you can and should pay yourself first. If you have had to take money out of a savings account to pay bills (not including emergencies), it may need to be lower. If you have not built up your "fun" fund savings account to treat yourself to some more expensive purchases, you may also want to lower it.

However, suppose you consistently have extra money left over each month after paying yourself first, taking care of your monthly bills, and contributing to your three savings accounts. In that case, you may need to increase the amount you pay yourself first. Remember, the purpose of paying yourself first is to make your future a priority without taking away from your current happiness. Don't beat yourself up if you are honestly living a frugal lifestyle and cannot pay yourself first with the amount you would like. It may mean you need to reevaluate your income streams (Mechanism 1) and expenses (Mechanism 2) to see where you can save more money.

Congratulations! You've just completed Freak Phase 10! It's time to be proud of your Freakishness and check in with your progress. Post a video of yourself describing the three most meaningful tasks you completed in this Freak Phase, and post a picture of yourself with your completed checklist from the beginning of this Phase.

Don't forget to use **#FREAKPHASE10** and **#TEENAGEFIFREAK** and to tag **@SHEEKSFREAKS** and **@BIGGERPOCKETS!**

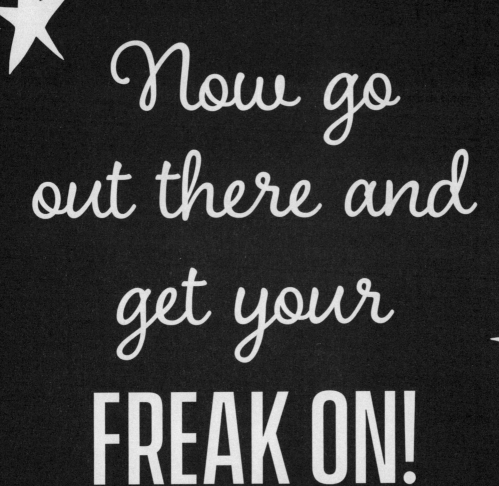

Now go out there and get your

FREAK ON!

FREAK PHASE *Eleven*

SEPTEMBER–DECEMBER
(If in college, first semester of sophomore year)

Income can be taken away and can come and go. Wealth, on the other hand . . . is much harder to lose, and in many cases, increases forever.

—SCOTT TRENCH, *SET FOR LIFE*

Here is the checklist for this four-month Freak Phase. It's best to read the entire Freak Phase before filling in the due date for each item. Don't forget to use your calendar to help you stay on track. And remember—you're a FI Freak, so you've got this!

DUE DATES	✓	TASK
	○	Read *Retire Early with Real Estate* by Chad Carson.
	○	Discuss your real estate investing ideas with your mentor.
	○	Establish criteria for your first real estate purchase.
	○	Go to three open houses.
	○	Meet with some lenders.
	○	Find the rest of your team.
	○	Set three financial goals.
	○	Implement a new Freak Tweak.
	○	Sell a personal item you no longer need or want.
	○	Find and do a new fun, free activity.
	○	Interview someone who is where you want to be.
	○	Evaluate your income streams.
	○	Calculate and track your net worth.
	○	Continue networking.
	○	Shadow someone for a day.

Goals
+ ACTION STEPS

DATE: _____

The date I communicated my three goals to my accountability partner.

Write out your three goals for this Freak Phase here.

1 ....

2 ....

3 ....

MY NEW "PAY YOURSELF FIRST"
PERCENTAGE
GOAL IS: ____ %

MY NEW
SAVINGS RATE
GOAL IS: ____ %

INTERVIEW Log

My New FREAK Tweak FOR FRUGALITY IS...

MONTH 1 / DATE COMPLETED

....

PERSON TO INTERVIEW

MONTH 2 / DATE COMPLETED

....

PERSON TO INTERVIEW

MONTH 3 / DATE COMPLETED

....

PERSON TO INTERVIEW

MONTH 4 / DATE COMPLETED

....

PERSON TO INTERVIEW

....

✦ Put a **RECURRING REMINDER** in your calendar to complete these tasks at the beginning of every Freak Phase.

Read *Retire Early with Real Estate* by Chad Carson

The author tells his story and gives excellent REI advice in this book. After graduating from college, Chad started wholesaling (a form of REI where an investor finds a distressed house and directly connects the seller and buyer, pocketing the profits) and never looked back. He was a hustler (another name for a FI Freak) and worked a ton of hours to get himself started on the right path. Plus, he practiced extreme frugality. His story is one example of how someone can reach FI at an early age.

Discuss Your Real Estate Investing Ideas with Your Mentor

In Phase 4, you found a mentor. Hopefully, you've developed a mutually beneficial relationship and a high level of trust with them. You should be connecting with your mentor at least twice a month. If you haven't already, schedule a meeting with your mentor (ideally in person) to discuss your REI plans.

Prepare for the meeting by organizing all your strategies and plans into a concise and easy-to-understand presentation. Tell your mentor all about your plan to house hack. Share what you've learned and the resources you've been using. Show them some of the numbers from properties you've analyzed.

Then ask them for their thoughts, ideas, and any feedback. If your mentor is also a real estate investor, they should have some great insights for you. *Write down* what they say. Ask them questions about anything you don't fully understand. Finally, as always, make sure you thank them for their time.

Write an outline of what you would like to cover with your mentor below.

Establish Criteria for Your First Real Estate Purchase

It's time to narrow down your criteria for your first house hack property. There are many types of house hacks, and Craig Curelop discusses a number of them in *The House Hacking Strategy* toward the end of Chapter Two.

For example, since many of you may be in college, you might want to buy a property that will house students. There are many pros and cons to owning such a property, and you should consider them all as you determine the criteria for your first purchase. If you're interested in this strategy, I highly recommend reading the two articles linked at biggerpockets.com/teenworkbook—you can also find a list of the many different types of house hacks at that link.

In addition to the type of house hack you'll pursue, you should know your criteria for the property itself. Things like the number of bedrooms, whether it should have a garage, and available parking are important. Use this list of questions to get you started in making your list of criteria:

What type of house hack do I want?

What is the most I'm willing to pay?

Can it be part of an HOA? (A Homeowner's Association is an organization that enforces rules and conducts maintenance in certain condos, townhomes, and subdivisions, often entailing a monthly or yearly HOA fee.)

What type of neighborhood am I looking for?

Does the property need to be near any businesses or highways?

How much work (repairs and upgrades) am I willing to complete and/or pay for?

How many units should the property have (if doing a small multifamily)?

How many bedrooms will the property have?

Does the property need to provide positive cash flow, or am I okay with just breaking even? ("Breaking even" means you are paying no rent yourself.)

What do I want the cash-on-cash return to be?

How old can the property be?

Does it need a garage? What would be enough parking?

How important is a yard?

Does it need to have air conditioning?

Should it have a basement?

Should it have the option to add more units, bedrooms, or bathrooms?

Any other requirements or wants?

Go to Three Open Houses

When you're ready to look at some properties that are actually for sale, you'll need to have a licensed agent with you. But there is one workaround—the open house. Pretty much anyone can tour a property when there is an open house. The seller's agent is "opening the house" for prospective buyers to take a look.

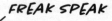

FREAK SPEAK

OPEN HOUSE: A planned event where prospective buyers can view a real estate property that is for sale without an appointment or accompanying agent.

You should take advantage of open houses during this Phase. Go to as many as you can, but visit at least three. Try your best to visit properties that meet many or most of your established criteria. But even if the property is not exactly what you want, you'll learn a lot of valuable information by touring in or near the area where you are looking to buy.

Visit biggerpockets.com/teenworkbook for an article about ways to find open houses near you and what to do when you get there, as well as a link to a YouTube video about avoiding mistakes when you do find the right property.

Meet with Some Lenders

The date of your first real estate purchase is getting closer and closer, so you need to do a few things to get ready for that milestone. None are quite as important as meeting with at least two lenders, because obtaining financing is the main roadblock for most young people seeking their first purchase. By meeting with a couple of lenders now, you can get ahead of the game and make sure that when the time comes, you'll be good to go.

Insufficient income history is the most common reason young people don't qualify for a mortgage. In Phase 6, you had the task of building a steady W-2 income history. In that Phase, we went over several ways to do this. The easiest solution (although it won't work for everyone) is to have a parent or other trusted adult co-sign on your mortgage. If that is not an option, you must prove to the lender that you can make your monthly mortgage payments by showing a sufficient income history.

If you are not a full-time student, hopefully you've spent the last year and a half (since Phase 6) working full-time for the same employer. If you are a full-time student, you probably haven't been working full-time. But, as I said in Phase 6, a part-time job over the same two-year period can sometimes do the trick.

Talking to a couple of lenders is essential because they can tell you exactly where you stand with your potential mortgage approval. If you are using a co-signer, lenders can let you know whether everything looks good with that path as well.

Getting Preapproved

Being preapproved for a mortgage means a lender believes your credit score, assets, income history, and debt-to-income ratio are satisfactory to receive a mortgage from their company. To get preapproved, talk to a lender and provide them with your financial information. I recommend doing this in person, if possible. Once you provide your information and discuss your goals with the lender, they will take a few days to look everything over and then let you know if you are preapproved.

You do *not* need to have a specific property in mind for this process, but lenders will want to know your estimated down payment. If you do not get preapproved, the lender will let you know why (if they don't, ask them), and you can work on fixing what needs to change.

Make sure you are getting *preapproved* and not *prequalified*. There is a difference. Getting prequalified is a much easier process, but it does not guarantee the lender will give you a loan when you need it.

To get preapproved, you must fill out a mortgage application. If you need help completing it, the lender will assist you. Some lenders may charge an application fee, which could be a few hundred dollars. Since you'll only complete a couple of applications for now, that should be okay.

For this step, you'll need to supply the lender with:
- Your Social Security number (so they can check your credit score)

- Your pay stubs for the last two months
- Recent bank statements for all your accounts
- Recent brokerage account statements
- In some cases, your last two years of income tax returns

If you have a co-signer, that person must be with you for all these steps. They will also have to supply their own records for all these items. Make sure you schedule a time that works for all three parties—the lender, the co-signer, and you.

Get these documents ready to go now. If needed, scan them so you can eventually email PDFs of each of these documents to the lender.

Who Should You Talk To?

I recommend you first contact the bank where you have your checking account. If you've had your account with a bank for a few years, that relationship can be a plus. Call up the nearest branch, make an appointment, and speak to a loan officer about getting preapproved for a mortgage.

 LOAN OFFICER: An employee of one lender who is paid a set salary (plus commissions). Loan officers can only offer loans from their employers.

For your second meeting, you should meet with a mortgage broker. A mortgage broker can look at loan offerings from many different lenders when finding loans for their clients.

 MORTGAGE BROKER: A middleman between you and potential lenders. The broker's job is to compare mortgage lenders on your behalf and find the best fit for you.

To find a mortgage broker, use your network. Ask people you know and trust if they can recommend a mortgage broker in the area where you'll be buying. If that doesn't turn up any leads, you could post a question on the BiggerPockets forums, where you'll likely receive some helpful replies and information.

Questions To Ask

When you talk to any potential lender, tell them precisely what you plan to do—house hack—then ask these questions:

- What interest rate do you think I will get? (Knowing this number will help you run more accurate analyses.)
- What do you think is the best loan option for me?
- Are there any current first-time homebuyer incentives?
- Are there any other opportunities you think I may be able to take advantage of?
- If my preapproval is denied, what can I do over the next few months to get approved?

Getting Denied

It's very possible you will not be preapproved. If so, insufficient income history could well be the reason. But that's why you are checking this out now. Ask the lender how much longer your income history needs to be and what you can do differently to get preapproved. Don't take the denial personally or let it dissuade you from your FI Freak journey. Your goal is to get preapproved when you're ready to buy that first property, not today.

Not being able to get preapproved at this stage is another one of those Freak Failures that will teach you something and benefit you in the long run. The first one or two or three lenders you talk to might turn you down. But that doesn't mean you will never get preapproved or should stop looking.

Go back to the series of videos from Jabbar on YouTube. In those videos, he documents his repeated failures at getting preapproved. He contacted thirteen lenders before finding one that preapproved him. He kept grinding until he solved the problem. Watch videos two through six to follow his journey. The link to those videos can be found at biggerpockets.com/teenworkbook.

Make a list here of lenders you will contact and write down what happens when you apply for pre-approval:

| NAME OF LENDER | NAME AND CONTACT INFO FOR PERSON I MET WITH | DATE | | RESULT |
		CONTACTED	OF MEETING	APPLIED FOR PREAPPROVAL	

One Final Crucial Tip

As you go from getting preapproved to closing on your first property, you will need to keep your credit score and debt levels in tip-top shape. Do *not* make any big financial changes or any significant purchases from now until you close on your first deal. That means *no* new credit cards or loans. And keep your bank account and brokerage account balances as high as they can be.

If anything changes in your financial picture, a lender can pull the plug on your preapproval, even at the last minute. You've done too much work for that to happen! Don't be the person who was about to close on a property, so they went to Home Depot to buy some new blinds. When the cashier asked if they would like to open a new Home Depot credit card so they could have zero percent interest for eighteen months, they said yes. That new credit card could be why the lender did not give them the loan to buy the house where the new interest-free blinds were supposed to be hung!

Finally, go to biggerpockets.com/teenworkbook for links to two podcast episodes about buying your first property and saving for your down payment that you should definitely check out.

Find the Rest of your Team

A common misconception . . . is that you need a full team before you start making offers on deals. This is a complete fallacy and is one of the biggest excuses for inaction. The only two team members you need before you start making offers on your first deal are an agent and a lender. Don't get me wrong: A good lawyer, accountant, and contractors are invaluable, but they can be sourced as needed. They are likely not necessary for your first deal.

—CRAIG CURELOP, "THE NEW INVESTOR'S SIMPLIFIED GUIDE TO LANDING A FIRST INVESTMENT PROPERTY," BIGGERPOCKETS BLOG

Throughout the many resources you've explored, you've certainly come across the idea of having a "team" working for you. This team is made up of people who will help you reach your goal of buying that first property. Your team may include:

- A lender
- A real estate agent or broker
- A maintenance person (handyperson)
- A contractor
- A property manager
- An accountant
- An attorney

Having knowledgeable people on your team can be invaluable. But you do *not* need to have all these team members in place to make your first house hack purchase.

As Craig Curelops says, you only need a lender and an agent to buy that first property. You'll find the other team members when you need them. It is *unnecessary* to have all these people in place to close on your first purchase. We will go over choosing a real estate agent in the next Phase, and we just got done talking about lenders. Let's talk briefly about the team members you don't yet need.

Maintenance Person (Handyperson)

You will probably need a good handyperson eventually, but not until you've closed on your first property and know what work needs to be done. You may even be able to do a lot of that work yourself. Perhaps you're comfortable painting, changing door locks, replacing a kitchen faucet, or installing blinds. If you're not but you're up for trying something new, you can learn how to do pretty much anything on YouTube. Handling some of the simpler stuff yourself can save some much-needed money during your first deal. For now, don't worry about finding a good handyperson.

Contractor

A contractor will complete renovations and upgrades to your property above and beyond what a maintenance person can do (think bathroom remodels or adding a new bedroom). If your property needs this kind of work, you'll cross this bridge when you get there. Again, you can wait on making this connection for now.

Property Manager

This one is simple. Since you'll be doing a house hack and living in the property yourself, you won't need a property manager for at least a year because you'll be managing the property while you live there. After a year, if you move out and no longer want to manage the property yourself, you can look for a property manager.

Accountant

Accountants are great for those who have multiple properties and want to seek professional advice about maximizing tax savings. For a new investor with one property, an accountant is overkill. When it comes time to file your income taxes for a year when you owned a property, you can seek the help of an income tax preparer. You don't need an accountant at this time.

Attorney

The same is true for an attorney. This is another team member you can wait on until you have a few properties.

Always Keep Your Ears Open

Just because you don't need some of these team members yet, that doesn't mean you should ignore any leads. If someone you know and trust recommends or even mentions a property manager or contractor they love, take note! Write down their name and contact information. When the time comes, having one or two names to start with will be a huge advantage.

CONGRATULATIONS!

You've just completed Freak Phase 11! It's time to be proud of your Freakishness and check in with your progress. Post a video of yourself describing the three most meaningful tasks you completed in this Freak Phase, and post a picture of yourself with your completed checklist from the beginning of this Phase.

Don't forget to use #FREAKPHASE11 and #TEENAGEFIFREAK and to tag @SHEEKSFREAKS and @BIGGERPOCKETS!

NOW GO OUT THERE
AND GET YOUR

FREAK
ON!

FREAK PHASE *Twelve*

JANUARY–APRIL
(If in college, second semester of sophomore year)

Anyone who has never made a mistake has never tried anything new.

—ATTRIBUTED TO ALBERT EINSTEIN

Here is the checklist for this four-month Freak Phase. It's best to read the entire Freak Phase before filling in the due date for each item. Don't forget to use your calendar to help you stay on track. And remember—you're a FI Freak, so you've got this!

DUE DATES	✓	TASK
	◯	Read *The 4-Hour Work Week* by Tim Ferriss.
	◯	Choose a real estate agent.
	◯	Determine your systems.
	◯	Open new bank accounts for your future property.
	◯	Start submitting offers.
	◯	Close on your first real estate purchase.
	◯	Set three financial goals.
	◯	Implement a new Freak Tweak.
	◯	Sell a personal item you no longer need or want.
	◯	Find and do a new fun, free activity.
	◯	Interview someone who is where you want to be.
	◯	Evaluate your income streams.
	◯	Calculate and track your net worth.
	◯	Continue networking.
	◯	Shadow someone for a day.

Goals +ACTION STEPS

The date I communicated my three goals to my accountability partner.

Write out your three goals for this Freak Phase here.

1 ....

2 ....

3 ....

MY NEW "PAY YOURSELF FIRST"
PERCENTAGE
GOAL IS: %

MY NEW
SAVINGS RATE
GOAL IS: %

INTERVIEW Log

MONTH 1 / DATE COMPLETED

....

PERSON TO INTERVIEW

....

MONTH 2 / DATE COMPLETED

....

PERSON TO INTERVIEW

....

MONTH 3 / DATE COMPLETED

....

PERSON TO INTERVIEW

....

MONTH 4 / DATE COMPLETED

....

PERSON TO INTERVIEW

....

My New FREAK Tweak

FOR FRUGALITY IS...

Put a **RECURRING REMINDER** in your calendar to complete these tasks at the beginning of every Freak Phase.

Read *The 4-Hour Work Week* by Tim Ferriss

In this book, which is super popular among FIRE community members, Tim Ferriss explains how to increase your income while decreasing your work hours. You won't be surprised to know that passive income plays an important role. The book gives inside information on building your life to run the way you've always wanted it to run. Buckle up for this read: It's got a ton of wisdom nuggets that will help you reach your goal of early FI.

Choose a Real Estate Agent

It's time to pick a real estate agent to work with for your house hack property purchase. This is a critical decision, and you want to pick the right person for you. You *don't* necessarily want to pick the easy option. For example, just because a relative or a friend is an agent, they are not necessarily the best choice. Yes, you may trust them because of your existing relationship, but if they are not savvy and experienced in finding properties that work for house hacking (or investment in general), they are likely *not* your best option.

Ideally, you want an agent who knows their stuff—one who has worked with investors, not just clients looking for a primary residence. Most agents fall into the latter category. They are great for someone who's buying a house to live in for the next five to twenty-five years. But *you* need an agent that is investor-friendly.

Use your network just like you did when looking for a lender. It's time to cash in on the relationships you've forged over the last few years. Let your core circle know you are looking for an agent. If that doesn't get you anywhere, reach out to the next layer of your networking circle. But be leery of posting a request for recommendations on social media platforms. If you do, multiple agents who may not be what you are looking for will respond.

Another place to find an investor-friendly agent is on the BiggerPockets website. You can search for agents in your area. Chances are they will be investor-friendly; otherwise, they wouldn't pay to have their information listed on the website. For a link to the agents on the BiggerPockets website, go to biggerpockets.com/agent/match.

There are many other tips and tricks to finding a great agent. Go back and review the advice from the books you've already read, including:

- Chapter Four of *The House Hacking Strategy* by Craig Curelop
- Chapter Four of *The Book on Rental Property Investing* by Brandon Turner
- Chapter Eight of *First-Time Home Buyer* by Scott Trench and Mindy Jensen

In addition, go to biggerpockets.com/teenworkbook for a link where you can watch or listen to a podcast episode focusing on other house hackers and how they chose their agents.

As you review these resources, jot down your main takeaways for finding the perfect real estate agent here ➡

NOTES ON FINDING THE PERFECT AGENT

Using all this wisdom and advice, you should have little problem finding the right agent. Don't be afraid to reject an agent if your gut is telling you no. Whoever you choose will be working *very* closely with you over the next few weeks to months. Do *everything* you can to make the best possible choice.

Finally, go to three more open houses in the area where you want to buy. You can do this either before or after you have chosen your agent.

Determine Your Systems

Your first property purchase is not far off! That means it's time to get two vital systems (game plans) in place to help guarantee success: your marketing system and your system for screening tenants.

Once you own your property and it's ready for tenants, you'll want to get rent-paying occupants moving in as soon as you can. But you want the *right* tenants. Having the *wrong* tenants can cause massive problems down the road. Get prepared now, so there's less to worry and think about when the time comes.

Review Chapters Nine through Eleven in *The House Hacking Strategy* by Craig Curelop. In those chapters, Craig covers everything you need to know. However, he covers systems for many different types of properties and strategies. Since you've already established *your* criteria, you know the type of property you're seeking to purchase and the strategies you'll use to make it work.

For even more information on screening tenants, go to biggerpockets.com/teenworkbook to listen to a podcast episode.

Use the space below to outline your systems for these two critical components.

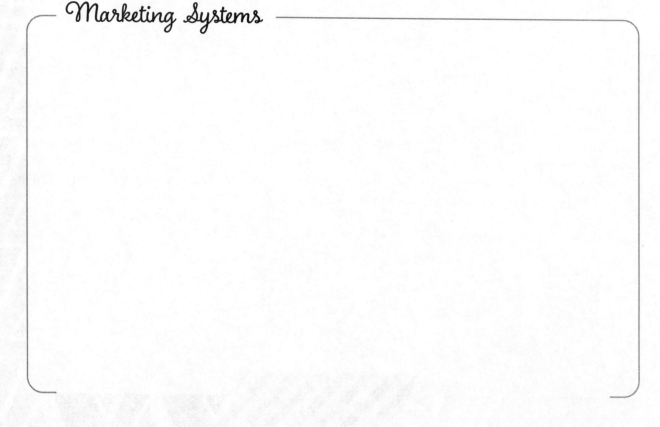

Marketing Systems

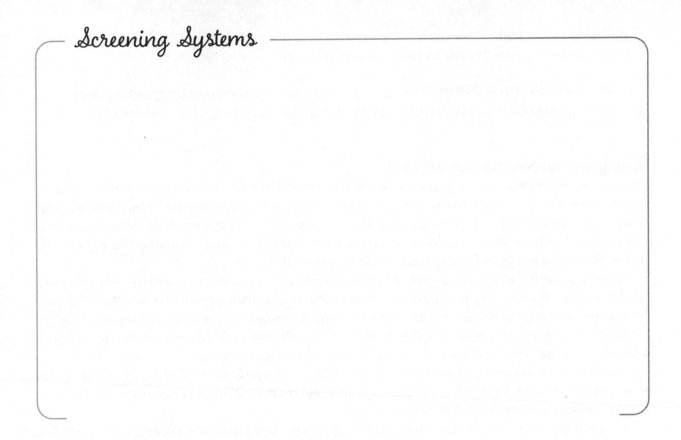

Open New Bank Accounts for Your Future Property

At this point, you should have at least one checking account and up to three savings accounts for your personal use. But they are for just that—personal use. If you keep the money related to your future investment property in those accounts, things will get blurry, and it will be difficult to know exactly how your investment is doing.

The solution is easy and usually free. (Most banks offer free checking and savings accounts.) You'll need to open another checking account and another savings account for the sole purpose of keeping your personal money and your business money separate. (Yes, owning a rental property is a business!) I recommend you open these new accounts at the same bank where you have your personal accounts. That way, you can instantly transfer money from one account to another using the bank's app.

Be aware that the accounts for your property do *not* have to be "business" accounts. Your bank will offer accounts specifically for businesses, but they usually have higher minimum balances and may not be free. Instead, open personal accounts. These will serve you just fine.

Call your bank and let them know you would like to open these two new accounts. You may be able to do it over the phone or online. If not, make an appointment to meet with a bank rep to get it done. Take the money out of your future investment savings account and transfer it into the new accounts. Putting $5,000 into the checking account and the rest into the new savings account is a good way to start.

By the way, most banks allow you to assign a name to your accounts. Take advantage of this feature to quickly and easily identify each account on your bank's app.

✦✚ Put a **RECURRING REMINDER** in your calendar to balance your checking and savings accounts every month, just as you do for your other bank accounts.

Managing Your New Savings Account

Properly managing your new savings account will be critical. It will hold the money you've saved for the down payment and closing costs (for now), money for initial repairs and upgrades (for now), your reserves for unexpected costs (I recommend $10,000–$15,000), money earmarked for capital expenditures (eventually), money earmarked for vacancies (eventually), money earmarked for repairs and maintenance (eventually), and extra money/cash flow (hopefully!).

As you can see, this new savings account has a lot going on. To know what money is for what purpose, you'll need to start a bookkeeping system. (Welcome to the world of owning your own business!) For your first property, this system does not have to be specialized, complicated, or even cost money. A simple spreadsheet, such as a Google Sheet, will be sufficient. You will need to visit the spreadsheet at least once a month to update the balance for each line item within the savings account.

As you know from having read a few books about REI, a rental property (including a house hack) will have several expenses. A few of these are not *regular* expenses but still must be accounted for. Here are the three main expenses that fall into this category:

- Capital expenditures (also known as CapEx): Expensive items that have to be replaced every few years—not every month or year—such as paint, carpet, appliances, furnace, or a roof.
- Vacancy expense: Income lost when no one is paying rent due to vacancy. This is an expense, not because you need to pay a bill, but because your expected income is reduced.
- Repairs and maintenance: Costs associated with keeping the property safe and in rent-ready condition, such as repairing plumbing and electrical, cleaning out the gutters, or replacing furnace filters.

When you analyze a potential property, you'll account for all the expected expenses of owning the property, including these three. The amount you'll need to plan on spending for these expenses can vary quite a bit. (See Chapter Five in *The Book on Rental Property Investing*.) Regardless of the amount you decide on, there will be some months when you don't have any CapEx, vacancy, or repair and maintenance expenses. When that happens, it doesn't mean the money you decided to set aside for those expenses goes into your pocket as extra cash flow. That money is meant to *accumulate* so that when one of those expenses does occur, you have the money to cover it.

Here's an example. Let's say your monthly rental income is $2,000 and you decide to put away 5 percent of that ($100 each month) to cover CapEx for one full year. If you had no such expenses during that year, you would have accumulated $1,200 in your savings account. Then, on December 31st, the furnace goes kaput, and you need to replace it ASAP. (It is winter, after all.) The replacement and installation of the furnace cost you $1,200. Congrats—you predicted your CapEx perfectly! But if you had spent or pocketed that earmarked money throughout the year, you would not have had enough saved to pay for the new furnace. You need to allow the money you set aside to accumulate, and you need to keep track of the amount.

Let's look at a more detailed example. Suppose you are about to buy property X. You've saved up enough money to buy it and have moved most of that money into a new savings account for property X. After analyzing the property, you know the following:

Cost of property	$200,000
Down payment	5 percent
Closing costs	$3,000
Initial repairs and upgrades	$5,000
Reserves	$10,000–$15,000
Monthly rent	$2,000
CapEx	5 percent of monthly rent
Vacancy	5 percent of monthly rent
Repairs and maintenance	5 percent of monthly rent

Note: You will pay your regular monthly expenses (mortgage payment, insurance, utilities, trash, etc.) out of your checking account, where you receive rents each month, so there is no need to accumulate money for those expenses in your savings account.

Let's imagine you close on the property on April 1st and get it rented on the same day. Let's also suppose that you had no CapEx, vacancy, or repairs/maintenance expenses for the first six months. With all this information, here is what your numbers would look like just before you bought the property (March 31st) and six months after buying it (September 30th).

Property X Savings Account Allocations

	March 31st	September 30th
Money for down payment	$10,000	$0
Money for closing costs	$3,000	$0
Money for initial repairs and upgrades	$5,000	$0
Reserves	$15,000	$15,000
CapEx	$0	$600
Vacancy	$0	$600
Repairs and maintenance	$0	$600
Total amount needed in account	$33,000	$16,800
Actual balance in account	$33,000	$17,500
Cash flow (available for withdrawal)	$0	$700

As you can see, each of the three non-regular expenses has an accumulated balance of $600. That money is waiting for a significant expense to hit, which *will* happen at some point.

When you do face an unexpected expense, let's say CapEx, and it is more than what you have saved, you can dip into your reserves to cover the cost. Then you would need to replenish the reserves while *also* contributing $100 per month to the CapEx "pot."

Use this list to get your new accounts set up quickly:

What bank will I use?	
What day did I open my new checking and savings accounts?	
How much did I put into my property's checking account?	
How much did I put into my property's savings account?	
Where is my savings account allocations spreadsheet saved?	

Start Submitting Offers

I have put this task and the next (close on your first real estate purchase) in Phase 12 for two reasons:

1. Unless you have a co-signer, this is the earliest you would be able to buy your first property. For those who are ready, I want you to have the information you need to make it a success.

2. If you are in college, you are nearing the end of your sophomore year. If your property will house you and some of your college friends, having it available before school finishes up this spring is essential, as many college students will sign leases for the following school year before leaving for the summer. Ideally, you want to time your purchase so that you can secure tenants before the end of the school year.

If you are not quite ready to buy your first property but are on a path to do so in the next couple of years, that's okay. When you do buy your first property, you'll be doing it in your early twenties. No matter how you look at it, that is pretty Freakish!

Buying real estate is a significant investment and should not be rushed into. However, you also don't want to lose a potential deal over something small that won't matter in the long run. Listen to your gut and remember that the real value of your first purchase is not the money or cash flow—it's everything you'll learn in the process.

If you have completed all the required tasks and are ready to find that first property, it's time to start *really* looking. Give your agent a call and tell them you are ready!

Also review the relevant chapters in these books and write down your main takeaways:

- Chapters Nine and Ten in *First-Time Home Buyer*
- Chapter Eight in *The House Hacking Strategy*
- Chapters Eleven and Twelve in *The Book on Rental Property Investing*

NOTES ON SUBMITTING OFFERS

_____

_____

_____

_____

_____

_____

_____

_____

_____

_____

_____

_____

_____

_____

Close on Your First Real Estate Purchase

This is it—the culmination of years of preparation, education, and planning! This is as good as it gets when it comes to Mechanism 4. But just a warning: The road to your first purchase could be bumpy. There will probably be some setbacks. Maybe you'll have a hard time getting an offer accepted. Maybe you'll face difficulties with financing. Maybe a deal will fall through at the last minute.

Encountering issues with your first purchase is another one of those Freak Failures: It will teach you something and benefit you in the long run. When trying to close on your first deal, remember that we must fail before we succeed. Whatever issues arise, lean on your agent, your mentor, and your network. They will support you and offer advice if needed. Be persistent and keep your head up. Millions before you have closed on their first property, and you will too! You've got this! You're a FI Freak!

Review the relevant chapters in these books:
- Chapters Eleven and Twelve in *First-Time Home Buyer*
- Chapter Eight in *The House Hacking Strategy*
- Chapter Sixteen in *The Book on Rental Property Investing*

As soon as you close on your first house hack property, go to the "Find Tenants and Start Managing Your Property" task in the next Freak Phase.

Finally, go to biggerpockets.com/teenworkbook for a link to a blog post titled "So, You Closed on Your First House Hack, Now What?" by Connor Anderson.

NOTES ON CLOSING ON YOUR FIRST DEAL

The day you close on your first property is a day you'll never forget! You definitely deserve to celebrate when it happens! Enjoy the fruits of your hard work.

And don't forget to post a picture of your property with **#FIFREAKPROPERTY1** and **#FREAKPHASE12** and to tag **@SHEEKSFREAKS** and **@BIGGERPOCKETS!**

NOW GO OUT THERE & GET YOUR FREAK ON!

FREAK PHASE *Thirteen*

MAY–AUGUST
(If in college, summer after sophomore year)

Don't ask yourself what the world needs. Ask yourself what makes you come alive, and then go do it. Because what the world needs is people who have come alive.

—HOWARD THURMAN

Here is the checklist for this four-month Freak Phase. It's best to read the entire Freak Phase before filling in the due date for each item. Don't forget to use your calendar to help you stay on track. And remember—you're a FI Freak, so you've got this!

DUE DATES	✓	TASK
	○	Read *Set for Life* by Scott Trench.
	○	Get your property ready to rent and find tenants.
	○	Conduct a thorough examination of your food costs.
	○	Review the amount you are paying yourself first.
	○	Set some real estate investing goals.
	○	Set three financial goals.
	○	Implement a new Freak Tweak.
	○	Sell a personal item you no longer need or want.
	○	Find and do a new fun, free activity.
	○	Interview someone who is where you want to be.
	○	Evaluate your income streams.
	○	Calculate and track your net worth.
	○	Continue networking.
	○	Shadow someone for a day.

Goals + ACTION STEPS

The date I communicated my three goals to my accountability partner.

Write out your three goals for this Freak Phase here.

1 ....

2 ....

3 ....

MY NEW "PAY YOURSELF FIRST"
PERCENTAGE GOAL IS:

%

MY NEW
SAVINGS RATE GOAL IS:

%

MONTH 1 / DATE COMPLETED

....

PERSON TO INTERVIEW

....

MONTH 2 / DATE COMPLETED

....

PERSON TO INTERVIEW

....

MONTH 3 / DATE COMPLETED

....

PERSON TO INTERVIEW

....

MONTH 4 / DATE COMPLETED

....

PERSON TO INTERVIEW

....

FOR FRUGALITY IS...

Put a **RECURRING REMINDER** in your calendar to complete these tasks at the beginning of every Freak Phase.

Read *Set for Life* by Scott Trench

This book is one of the reasons I wrote *First to a Million*. After reading *Set for Life*, I became even more adamant about spreading the message of early FI. Scott's book has changed many people's lives for the better, but it was written for someone who's at least in their late twenties. As a high school teacher who prefers to advocate for teens, I knew they needed a book written just for them.

Most people in our country believe there is only one option—to work until they're 65 and then retire. *Set for Life* makes it absolutely clear that other options exist and are not impossible or even difficult. *Set for Life* has many lessons, strategies, and tactics that will pertain to you and your journey. Enjoy!

Get Your Property Ready to Rent and Find Tenants

You should start working on this task as soon as you close on your first property. You'll begin by managing any initial repairs, maintenance, or upgrades that must be completed before tenants can move in.

At the end of this task, fill in the list of everything you want to fix or upgrade. Then, carefully go through that list and cross off everything that isn't necessary. Most new homeowners incorrectly believe everything must be perfect with their property. *Not true!* Does the kitchen really need new paint? Does the bedroom really need a ceiling fan installed? Does the garage door really have to be replaced right now? Many (or perhaps most) of the things on your list would be nice but are not necessary.

Remember, you are running a business. Every dollar you spend is a dollar out of your pocket or a dollar that cannot be invested elsewhere. You need to take your Freakish frugal habits and apply them to your new property. Complete only the repairs and upgrades necessary to provide a safe and clean property with just a few extras to make it stand out to prospective tenants. In short, don't let the excitement of owning your first property allow you to forget about Mechanism 2. Even though you are dealing with your first house hack today, you need to be thinking of your next purchase. Saving money and earning extra income are crucial to allow you to make that next purchase in just a year.

Now that you've crossed several items off your list, go through the remaining items and decide what you'll do yourself, what you'll hire a handyperson to do, and what you may need a contractor to complete. You can take care of many tasks yourself, even if you are not very handy. Search YouTube for "How do I replace a toilet?" or "How do I change the locks?" or "How do I install new light fixtures?" You'll be surprised at how easy some of these things are and how much money you can save by doing them yourself.

A handyperson or a contractor will have to take care of any other items on your to-do list. The big items—such as adding a new bathroom, replacing the roof, or remodeling the kitchen—are for contractors. If you have something big on your to-do list, start searching for a contractor right away. Good contractors are busy and may not be able to get to your project as quickly as you hope, so start calling contractors for bids now.

For all the items that are not do-it-yourself or contractor assignments, a handyperson will do. Here are some apps you can use to find and book a reputable handyperson:
- Thumbtack
- TaskRabbit
- Porch
- Handy

Getting tenants moved in as quickly as possible is crucial, since every day that goes by costs you money in the form of lost rental income. The first month or two you own your property will likely be insanely busy as you get it up and running. This is where the rubber meets the road. But you've been planning for this for years. So power through and know that decades of your future time will be the reward for all your hard work. Employ the systems you designed in Phase 12 to market your property and find quality tenants.

Review these relevant chapters to help you effectively manage your new property:
- Chapters Seventeen and Eighteen in *The Book on Rental Property Investing*
- Chapter Thirteen in *First-Time Home Buyer*
- Chapter Twelve in *The House Hacking Strategy*

Make a list here of the things you want to fix or upgrade:

WHAT NEEDS TO BE FIXED OR UPDATED?	DO IT MYSELF, HANDYPERSON, OR CONTRACTOR?

Conduct a Thorough Examination of Your Food Costs

Goldilocks expressed it well when she declared the porridge not too hot, not too cold, but just right. Frugality is something like that— not too much, not too little, but just right. Nothing is wasted or left unused . . . It's that magic word—enough.

—VICKI ROBIN AND JOE DOMINGUEZ , *YOUR MONEY OR YOUR LIFE*

Now that you are house hacking, you have completed a monumental step toward eliminating your housing expenses. Great work! As you may remember, housing expenses are the costliest expenditure for most Americans. Since you have Freakishly eliminated (or significantly reduced) housing expenses from your life, we should review another one of the top three expenses for Americans: food.

The last time we talked about food costs was in Phase 7, where we examined your new budget since you had just graduated from high school. Now that a couple of years have gone by, let's check in with how well you're using Mechanism 2 on your food costs. Ask yourself these questions:

- How often do I eat out, get takeout, or have food delivered?
- When I do eat out, what types of restaurants do I choose, and how do I choose what to order?
- Do I waste food? Am I throwing away expired or rotten food?
- What grocery stores do I shop at? Are there others that are less expensive?
- When I go grocery shopping, do I have a list? If so, do I stick to it?
- Do I plan my meals?
- Do I search online for less expensive recipes and meal options?

Do not hold yourself to a standard of spending as little on food as you possibly can. That's not healthy for several reasons. However, do examine your answers to those questions and think about ways to cut back on costs without giving up anything you value.

For example, if you currently eat out five times a week on average, would your overall happiness suffer if you dropped to four times a week? If you could save $50 a week by driving a little further to a less expensive grocery store, is that something you might consider?

Make a Meal Plan for a Week and Shop for Your Food Intentionally

One strategy you can try (if you don't do this already) is to make a weekly meal plan. This involves sitting down for about thirty minutes to plan your meals and snacks for a week. For instance, on Friday nights, try planning all your meals for the next week. While you're at it, search online for recipes that sound yummy but are low cost. Take your frugality one step further by planning your meals based on upcoming weekly deals or bargains being promoted at your favorite grocery store.

FREAK TECHNIQUE **MEAL PLANNING:** Planning out your weekly meals in order to save time and money while also eating a healthier diet.

You can save money through meal planning by:

- Finding lower-cost meal options
- Learning which meals can be stretched into two days or last longer in the fridge as leftovers
- Not going out to eat as much because "there's nothing to eat at home"
- Sticking to your shopping list and not making impulse purchases

Take thirty minutes to plan your meals for one week. Write down what each meal will be as well as what items you'll need to prepare them and in what amount. Then shop *only* for what's on your list. After the week is over, compare your food expenses for the week you planned to your weekly food expenses over the previous two months. (I hope you're still tracking all your income and expenses!)

Go back to biggerpockets.com/teenworkbook and Phase 7 for links to helpful resources.

Write down your meal plan here:

SUNDAY	BREAKFAST
	LUNCH
	DINNER

MONDAY	BREAKFAST
	LUNCH
	DINNER

TUESDAY	BREAKFAST
	LUNCH
	DINNER

WEDNESDAY

BREAKFAST

....

LUNCH

....

DINNER

THURSDAY

BREAKFAST

....

LUNCH

....

DINNER

FRIDAY

BREAKFAST

....

LUNCH

....

DINNER

SATURDAY

BREAKFAST

....

LUNCH

....

DINNER

Review the Amount You Are Paying Yourself First

If you're following the workbook, you've been paying yourself first every month like a true FI Freak. However, the last time you reviewed the amount you pay yourself first was in Phase 10. If you did buy your first house hack property in Phase 12, your monthly budget and expenses have changed quite a bit. Now that you've greatly reduced or eliminated your housing expenses, there's probably a lot more money you could be paying yourself first.

Take three months to get used to your new financial picture. After analyzing your income and expenses for those three months, reevaluate the percentage you are paying yourself first. At the beginning of the *First to a Million* workbook (in Phases 2 and 3), we set the benchmark at 30 percent. You should now be able to increase that substantially, thus growing your savings and future investments! Many house hackers have savings rates in the 60 to 80 percent range or even higher. Choose a new percentage that maximizes Mechanisms 3 and 4 *and* allows you to have balance, value, and happiness in your life.

MY "PAY YOURSELF FIRST" PERCENTAGE GOAL FOR EACH MONTH IN THIS PHASE IS:

%

Set Up an Auto Transfer to Your Future Investment Savings Account

If you have a steady income from a full- or part-time job, consider setting up an auto transfer from your checking account into your future investment savings account each pay period. (You may have already set this up.) The only exception will be if you foresee your income either decreasing or ceasing in the near future.

The amount you automatically transfer should be the amount you pay yourself first. Setting up an auto transfer for that amount a few days after each paycheck is deposited makes it easier not to spend that money on something else. This is because when people see money in their checking account, they tend to think it's money to be spent. Just remember to set up the auto transfer for three or four days after your paychecks are deposited to allow time for the deposit to clear.

See the "Open a Brokerage Account" task in Freak Phase 4.5 for more detailed instructions.

Set Some Real Estate Investing Goals

By now you've read several books on REI and how it can maximize Mechanism 4. You've also listened to several podcasts and read many articles about REI. Some of you even own your first real estate investment. All the knowledge you have, combined with the experience you are now gaining, makes this a perfect time to take an in-depth look at your future REI goals.

Begin by being honest with yourself about how much you do or don't enjoy REI. It's not for everybody. For those who don't enjoy the hands-on approach to REI, there are other options for taking advantage of this amazing strategy, such as investing in a REIT (real estate investment trust), a real estate mutual fund, or crowdfunding opportunities.

Some Freaks get hooked on REI before they've even closed on their first property. Making that purchase only feeds their infatuation with the potential of REI. If you fall into this category, I'd like to take a minute to give you fair warning.

Real estate is a fantastic way to invest and build wealth—you'll get no argument from me on that point. But I have seen many FI Freaks take it to an unhealthy extreme. In short, REI can become all-consuming, almost addictive, and some investors find themselves buying as much real estate as they possibly can.

As you get started with REI, ask yourself the following:

- Since REI is not 100 percent passive, how much time am I willing to spend on REI versus items on my happiness list?
- How important is it to me, if at all, that I can brag about how big my real estate portfolio is or how many properties I buy each year?
- If happiness and freedom of time are the ultimate goals of early FI, how will REI fit into my best life?

I've seen numerous FI Freaks and others fall victim to the lure of REI. Acquiring more and more properties slowly replaces the goal of being happy and free. Remember, the goal is to escape or avoid the rat race of *having* to work. But REI can quickly turn from a mostly passive investment strategy into a full-time job.

Many of the podcasts, books, articles, and videos you'll navigate while pursuing early FI can make it seem like you need to own dozens or even hundreds of properties. *Not true!* In fact, you may only need to own a few properties to reach early FI—*if* they are great properties.

At some point, enough is enough. Don't let other people persuade you into thinking you *need* to get bigger. Don't get caught up in other people's goals or what they say you should be doing. It's not a competition. You don't need to have more properties or real estate equity than the person next to you. The goal is not to be the person with the most investment properties or the most wealth. **The goal is to have the freedom and flexibility to do the things on your happiness list.**

Maybe building a real estate empire to grow your net worth to extremely high levels is one of the things that will bring you happiness. If you enjoy building your portfolio and managing all its components, there's nothing wrong with that. But only do it knowing you are creating a job for yourself (even if you use property managers) when the whole idea from the beginning was to *not* have to work.

Jot down some REI goals for the next five years ➡

MY REAL ESTATE INVESTING GOALS
FOR THE NEXT FIVE YEARS:

_____

_____

_____

_____

_____

_____

_____

_____

_____

_____

_____

_____

_____

_____

Congratulations!

You've just completed Freak Phase 13! It's time to be proud of your Freakishness and check in with your progress. Post a video of yourself describing the three most meaningful tasks you completed in this Freak Phase, and post a picture of yourself with your completed checklist from the beginning of this Phase.

Don't forget to use **#FREAKPHASE13** and **#TEENAGEFIFREAK** and to tag **@SHEEKSFREAKS** and **@BIGGERPOCKETS!**

Now Go Out There & Get Your FREAK ON!

FREAK PHASE *Fourteen*

SEPTEMBER–DECEMBER
(If in college, first semester of junior year)

One of the really great things about being [financially independent] is the ability to help others. Over the years, I have noticed that many of the richest people in the world give money away. To be truly rich, we need to be able to give as well as to receive. Giving money away is one of the best ways to help right the wrongs of the world. It's a wonderful feeling to see a problem and know that you have the power to donate the money to a cause or group that will help make the world a better place. Buying things for yourself is great but giving money to others is the best feeling in the world. Try it! You'll get an idea of the true power of money.

—ROBERT KIYOSAKI, *RICH DAD POOR DAD FOR TEENS*

Here is the checklist for this four-month Freak Phase. It's best to read the entire Freak Phase before filling in the due date for each item. Don't forget to use your calendar to help you stay on track. And remember—you're a FI Freak, so you've got this!

DUE DATES	✓	TASK
	◯	Read *Financial Freedom* by Grant Sabatier.
	◯	Compare rates from different car insurance companies.
	◯	Continue to avoid lifestyle inflation.
	◯	Get ready to buy your second property.
	◯	Plan for the remainder of your early FI journey.
	◯	Set three financial goals.
	◯	Implement a new Freak Tweak.
	◯	Sell a personal item you no longer need or want.
	◯	Find and do a new fun, free activity.
	◯	Interview someone who is where you want to be.
	◯	Evaluate your income streams.
	◯	Calculate and track your net worth.
	◯	Continue networking.
	◯	Shadow someone for a day.

Goals +ACTION STEPS

DATE: _____

The date I communicated my three goals to my accountability partner.

Write out your three goals for this Freak Phase here.

1 ....

2 ....

3 ....

MY NEW "PAY YOURSELF FIRST"
PERCENTAGE GOAL IS:

%

MY NEW
SAVINGS RATE GOAL IS:

%

FOR FRUGALITY IS...

MONTH 1 / DATE COMPLETED

....

PERSON TO INTERVIEW

....

MONTH 2 / DATE COMPLETED

....

PERSON TO INTERVIEW

....

MONTH 3 / DATE COMPLETED

....

PERSON TO INTERVIEW

....

MONTH 4 / DATE COMPLETED

....

PERSON TO INTERVIEW

....

Put a **RECURRING REMINDER** in your calendar to complete these tasks at the beginning of every Freak Phase.

Read *Financial Freedom* by Grant Sabatier

Financial Freedom is a guide to making more money in less time. Its primary purpose is to give the reader the tools and insight needed to have more time for the things they love. This book challenges the traditional American Dream path and instead offers readers an alternative: Choose to live differently so you can achieve early FI and live your best life.

When the author, Grant Sabatier, was 25 he had less than $5 in his bank account. Just five years later, he had a net worth of more than $1.25 million. Soon after, he reached FI. During his Freakish journey, he discovered that most of the accepted wisdom about money, work, and retirement is incorrect, incomplete, or too old-school for today's FI Freaks.

Compare Rates from Different Car Insurance Companies

Car insurance can be super expensive when you are young. Therefore, researching your best option for car insurance is essential for maximizing Mechanism 2. Let's first take a look at whose insurance policy you should be on. Then we'll examine how to find the least expensive option.

How Your Specific Situation Affects Your Options

Including the car you drive on your parents' car insurance policy is almost always the best choice when it comes to saving money. If you can legally include your car on their policy, you should. More than likely, this is the best option whether your parents are generous enough to pay your insurance or whether you pay your own share.

Here is a breakdown of what you're allowed to do in various situations, according to Progressive.

- You can share an auto policy with your parents if your vehicle is kept overnight at your parents' address. If you live and park your vehicle at a different address than your parents, you need your own policy.
- In most states, the car's registered owner doesn't have to match the name on the insurance policy. That means a car in your name can be insured on your parents' policy. However, some states require that the name on the vehicle registration match the name on the auto insurance policy. In these states you must have your own auto policy.
- If you move out of state with your vehicle, you need a new auto policy for that state. However, most states permit you to stay on your parents' policy while you attend a college or university out of state—depending on the state and depending on the ZIP code where your car is kept. If you're living off-campus year-round in a separate address from your parents, you need your own auto policy.[1]

Since some states (and some insurance providers) have different rules, the best way to determine the exact guidelines for your situation is to talk to a car insurance representative. Begin by calling the company you currently use and asking questions that pertain to your situation.

---

1 "How Long Can Children Stay On Their Parents' Insurance?" Progressive.com, Progressive, accessed July 16, 2021, https://www.progressive.com/answers/staying-on-your-parents-insurance/.

YES	NO	
○	○	If I live with my parents, can I stay on their policy?
○	○	Does my state require the car to be registered to the same person as the policy?
○	○	If I am attending college out of state, can I stay on my parents' policy?

Using this information, determine if you'll stay on your parents' policy or need to get your own. If you cannot stay on your parents' policy, this next section is especially important.

How To Find The Best Rates

If, or when, you need to find your own policy, there are some steps and strategies you can use to find the best rate. But I will be honest with you up front: Completing this task will take some time, and comparing auto insurance policies is no fun. However, if you can find a policy that is just $50 less per month, that adds up to $600 a year! So, even though it may take you half a day to get and compare quotes from three car insurance companies, the additional savings can be worth it. Set aside a half day during this Phase to complete this task. Your future self will thank you.

First, find out what coverage you currently have so you can get estimates for policies with the same coverage. That way you are comparing apples to apples. To see the exact coverage you have now, look at your insurance policy—the details will be listed on the invoice. To find the most recent invoice, you may need to log into the company's website or call and request that one be emailed to you.

Next, gather some information. To get an accurate quote from other insurance companies, you'll need the following:

- Driver name and date of birth
- Driver's license number and issuing state
- Vehicle Information Number (VIN)
- Current mileage on your car
- Address where the vehicle is registered
- Name of the registered owner
- Prior insurance carrier and expiration date
- Vehicle's date of purchase
- What you use the vehicle for (work or leisure)
- Driving records of all drivers listed on the policy

Third, when asking for quotes, be on the lookout for possible discounts. Here are the most common discounts available to young people:

- Accident-free or safe driver discounts
- Low-mileage discount (if you don't drive your car very much)

- Good-student discount (if you have a B average or better)
- Homeowner discount (a benefit of owning that house hack!)

Many websites will show you quotes from different car insurance companies; you can find them with a quick Google search. You can also visit the website of most car insurance companies and get a free quote by entering your information. Again, this is not exciting stuff. But saving and investing an extra $600 or more is!

MY CURRENT COVERAGE	QUOTES FROM THREE COMPANIES
	COMPANY 1
MY INFORMATION	COMPANY 2
MY POSSIBLE DISCOUNTS	COMPANY 3

Continue to Avoid Lifestyle Inflation

One of the best pieces of advice I ever actually received was to live like a college student for as long as you possibly can. College is some of the most fun times in life, but I don't think many of us had a lot of disposable income, so just because you have a paycheck doesn't mean you should start spending money wildly.

—DREW FROM GUY ON FIRE, *BIGGERPOCKETS MONEY PODCAST,* EPISODE 9

At some point over the next few years, you'll find yourself earning and saving more money than you ever have before. You may be at that point today, or it may happen in the near future, once you graduate from college and get a full-time job. Whatever the case, it is crucial to keep your spending constant while your income increases. A speedy road to early FI depends on it.

Over the last few years, you've been working diligently on all four Mechanisms. But the truth is those years were just practice for the two or three years to come. Building wealth is progressive—think of it like a train gaining momentum over time. You've put in a huge amount of work to get the heavy locomotive of FI moving forward. If you now focus on preventing lifestyle inflation for the next few years, the train will continue to gain speed, accelerating your journey to early FI.

When you have all the following components, your early FI journey is advancing full steam ahead. Check off the ones that apply to you:

✓	TASK
○	Housing expenses are incredibly low or eliminated (house hacking).
○	Transportation expenses are incredibly low or eliminated.
○	Food costs are low.
○	You are working a full-time job.
○	You have a successful side hustle or two.
○	You have at least one form of passive income other than real estate.
○	You are consistently investing money in index funds and/or real estate.

These steps keep the train of FI on its tracks. You may already be seeing the astonishing effects of your financial momentum. Or you may still be a year or two away. When you do see it working, it's impressive. And it will continue to vigorously build momentum, increasing exponentially, *if* you allow it to by avoiding lifestyle inflation.

Continue to balance frugality with happiness and future goals with immediate gratification. Keep true to your journey, and don't get off-track. Remember, early FI will come earlier *without* lifestyle inflation.

Get Ready to Buy Your Second Property

To buy your first property, you needed four things:

1. Cash
2. Knowledge
3. Excellent credit score
4. Income history

As you start planning to buy your second, you'll notice the list is not as daunting. Items 2 and 3 are still in place. Item 4 should not have changed. But item 1—that's a different story.

The best-case scenario is to buy your second property precisely a year after you bought your first and house hack the second one too. You'll need about the same amount of cash saved in your future investment savings account for your second purchase as you needed for your first. The total must cover:

- Down payment
- Closing costs
- Initial repairs and upgrades
- Reserves ($10,000–$15,000)

This is one reason why avoiding lifestyle inflation and continuing to be frugal are so essential. If you are not on pace to save this money in time to buy your next property at exactly the one-year mark, that's okay. Hopefully it will not be too far after that. Can you make some adjustments now to help yourself reach your goal?

Based on the amount you currently have saved for your next purchase, your savings rate, and the amount you think you'll need, try to predict when your next purchase will happen. Then, start connecting with your lender and agent a couple of months before to start planning the purchase of your second property.

Without a doubt, you've gained an incredible amount of knowledge since you started looking for your first property. Going through the processes of finding a lender and agent, searching for properties, putting in offers, negotiating with the seller, closing on the deal, making repairs to the property, getting it rent-ready, finding and screening tenants, and managing the property have undeniably taught you more than any book, podcast, or YouTube video ever could.

With all this new knowledge and valuable experience, your next purchase will be much easier than the first. And your third purchase will be even easier than the second. Then you're off and running toward building a real estate investment portfolio!

ESTIMATED AMOUNT NEEDED TO BUY PROPERTY NO. 2

Estimated Down Payment	$
Estimated Closing Costs	$
Estimated Initial Repairs and Upgrades	$
Estimated Reserves	$
TOTAL ESTIMATED AMOUNT NEEDED TO PURCHASE	$
Minus Amount Already Saved For Future Real Estate Investments	— $
ESTIMATED AMOUNT STILL NEEDED	$
Divided by the Number of Months Till I Want to Buy Property No. 2	$
AMOUNT NEEDED TO SAVE EACH MONTH	$

Plan for the Remainder of Your Early FI Journey

The reason [financially independent] people work so hard is because they no longer need to work for money. They work to solve a problem they are passionate about, master a hobby they enjoy, or to build a business . . . Because they have total control over how they spend their time, they only participate in projects that are truly interesting and engaging to them.

—SCOTT TRENCH, *SET FOR LIFE*

In my opinion, the primary purpose of reaching early FI is to have more time to do the things that bring you happiness. Look at your happiness list. (You should be updating it once a year.) Are you finding time to enjoy those things while on your journey to early FI? Are you taking the time to do those things more often? Review why you're following this journey in the first place. Early FI will come. You'll get there. But what does that mean, and what will you do once you're there? The moment you satisfy the FI Equation, you are financially free. But what then?

Building Your Investments

When you do satisfy the FI Equation, you won't just stop. The journey continues, but on *your* terms. You'll continue to grow your investments (Mechanism 4) to strengthen your position and build wealth.

Investing more in index funds is smart and simple. Remember, index fund investing, like all investing, is long-term. When you initially reach FI, it will be due largely—if not entirely—to your passive income streams and your low living expenses. Sustainable asset withdrawal usually does not play a significant role for those who reach FI very early in life. It will, however, play a prominent role a few decades down the road. Knowing that, continue investing in index funds according to your investing ratio.

How you continue to invest in real estate over the next few years is a whole other story. As you've learned along your journey so far, there are numerous ways to invest in real estate. While house hacking is by far the best strategy for new and young investors, you'll eventually be able to try out some other REI strategies to build your wealth. Perhaps you'll delve into one of these options:

- The BRRRR method
- Out-of-state investing
- Multifamily properties
- Short-term rentals
- Fix and flips
- Live-in fix and flips
- Turnkey investing
- 1031 exchanges

Once you reach early FI, continuing to apply all four Mechanisms while investing more in index funds and real estate will be the best way to increase your wealth and live your best life.

Growing Your Real Estate Portfolio

Adding more cash-flowing properties to your real estate portfolio is a strategy you'll likely pursue in one way or another. For now, you can achieve this by investing in another house hack every year or so. Each time you do, you increase your passive income, making it easier and faster to save up for your next purchase.

Eventually, you'll get to a point where you have enough cash saved to buy a property that is not a house hack. You'll even be able to put down at least 20 percent for the purchase. If the numbers work, investing in more real estate properties is a tried-and-true wealth-building tactic you should absolutely pursue.

If you do decide to pursue it, set a goal to reach $5,000 a month in passive income from your real estate investments, including your house hacks. For a detailed description of several wealth-building options for REI, review Chapters Fifteen through Eighteen in Chad Carson's book *Retire Early with Real Estate*.

Your Living Expenses Will Eventually Increase

Although we've talked extensively about avoiding lifestyle inflation and remaining frugal, you'll eventually want to increase your living expenses. This may happen because of getting married, starting a family, or just deciding that house hacking is no longer providing a value that outweighs the drawbacks of that strategy.

There will come a point when you'll want to spend more on travel or food. You might want to purchase a nicer car (do *not* finance it!) or some newer tech devices. There is nothing wrong with enjoying the fruits of your labor down the road. Just remember to always ask yourself, "Do I find value in this purchase?" Increasing your living expenses does not mean you should start spending lavishly. You can quickly lose ground on your journey if you spend frivolously.

Different levels of frugality work well with different stages of your journey, but one thing remains constant: Spending on things you don't value is not a good use of your hard-earned money. It is best to maintain your frugal lifestyle even through the first few years of FI.

An expense that *should* increase over time is the amount of money you put away in reserves—your "just in case" savings. Once you reach FI and see your wealth growing more rapidly, you'll need to begin planning for more risks. After reaching FI, you have more to lose. Therefore, you should start planning for threats to your wealth. What happens if there is an economic crisis, recession, real estate market collapse, world pandemic, or some other unforeseen catastrophe? One of the best ways to protect against such events destroying your wealth is to have larger cash reserves.

Having cash saved or safely invested (in bonds, CDs, or just a high-interest savings account) is an intelligent way to safeguard against these types of events so they don't ruin your financial position. Somewhere around the time you reach FI, begin putting more money into your reserves.

Once You've Reached FI

There's no feeling quite like freedom—the freedom to do what you want, when you want, with whom you want. While there are many benefits to reaching early FI, the freedom to enjoy your life on your own terms is hard to beat.

Whenever you reach that point, I have one thing to say: Congratulations! Achieving FI at a young age is truly a Freakish accomplishment. Getting there involves years of hard work and, at times, sacrifice. It involves risk, courage, and ignoring the naysayers. It is an accomplishment that others will see as remarkable and extraordinary.

At that point, you will have joined the ranks of a select group of young people who are financially independent.

Initially, reaching FI allows you to move forward without doing things you hate. (If you hate your full-time job, you can now quit!) But you'll need to continue to build wealth, investments, and passive income—in a way you enjoy—so you can eventually increase your spending without moving backward. Find a way to build wealth that is fulfilling. It could be growing a side hustle, starting a small business, continuing to build your real estate portfolio, or working a part-time job you love.

Thanks to the vast amounts of free time you now have available, you can also choose to dedicate part of your life to something you believe is more important than your individual existence. Your higher-level whys can start to become a reality. Maybe you'll start a business that focuses on one of your passions. Maybe you'll work for a nonprofit that helps a cause near and dear to your heart. Maybe you'll regularly volunteer for a local charity. Giving back is one of the main benefits of reaching early FI, so enjoy it!

Conclusion

You probably first picked up *First to a Million* more than five years ago. And now you are at the end of the *First to a Million* workbook. Think back to where you were five years ago. Other than being five years younger, what else was different?

Today you have a brokerage account with growing investments in index funds—the best way to invest in the stock market. You have an extensive network of friends and connections who share your mentality. You own a real estate investment property (or you will soon). You live frugally while saving money, resources, and energy. You have several bank accounts and manage them intelligently. You have a plan for your financial future. You know what brings you the most happiness. You have multiple streams of income, many of which are passive. You believe in yourself and are confident you can do anything—*and you will*. You are a FI Freak.

I'm sure my book and my workbook were not perfect road maps for your journey. I'm sure your journey has had its ups and downs. I'm sure there are many failures in your future. This is life. It is beautiful and fulfilling and magnificent. And you can now enjoy every second of it, having the freedom to do what you want as a FI Freak.

I once heard a renowned speaker talk about leadership. He was 70 years old and had traveled the world, acquired two doctorates, and spent countless hours working with college students. He gave a great speech, but one quote stuck with me, and it is very fitting at this time:

"SHIPS ARE SAFE IN THE HARBOR, BUT THAT'S NOT WHAT THEY WERE BUILT FOR."

You are the ship and your mast of full of wind. You must leave the harbor because that is what you were built for. Test the waters, travel to beautiful places, encounter extraordinary people, and explore your life.

Thank you for being the incredible young person you are, and for all the good you'll do in the world. To close, I could wish you good luck, but you don't really need it. Instead, I'll say "Enjoy the ride," because you have many more great memories, challenges, and accomplishments waiting for you—and these will take you further than even you can imagine. I wish you peace and blessings always as you continue your Freakish journey!

CONGRATS!

You've just completed Freak Phase 14 and the First to a Million Workbook! It's time to be proud of your Freakishness and check in with your progress. Post a video of yourself describing the three most meaningful tasks you completed in this Freak Phase, and post a picture of yourself with your completed checklist from the beginning of this Phase.

Don't forget to use **#FREAKPHASE14** and **#TEENAGEFIFREAK** and to tag **@SHEEKSFREAKS** and **@BIGGERPOCKETS!**

FREAK

NOW GO OUT THERE AND GET YOUR

ON!

More from
BiggerPockets Publishing

If you enjoyed this book, we hope you'll take a moment to check out some of the other great material BiggerPockets offers. BiggerPockets is *the* real estate investing social network, marketplace, and information hub, designed to help make you a smarter real estate investor through podcasts, books, blog posts, videos, forums, and more. Sign up today—it's free! **Visit www.BiggerPockets.com.**

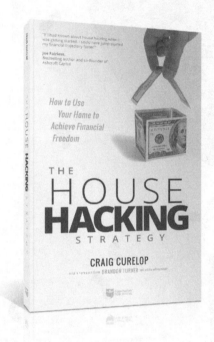

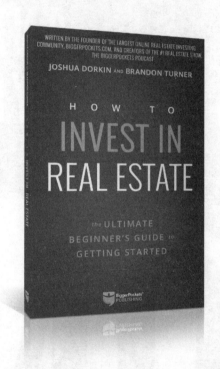

The House Hacking Strategy

Don't pay for your home. Hack it and live for free! When mastered, house hacking can save you thousands of dollars in monthly expenses, build tens of thousands of dollars in equity each year, and provide the financial means to retire early. Discover why so many successful investors support their investment careers with house hacking—and learn from a frugality expert who has "hacked" his way toward financial freedom.

How to Invest in Real Estate

Two of the biggest names in the real estate world teamed up to write the most comprehensive manual ever written on getting started in the lucrative business of real estate investing. Joshua Dorkin and Brandon Turner give you an insider's look at the many different real estate niches and strategies so that you can find which one works best for you, your resources, and your goals.

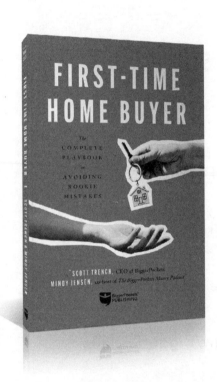

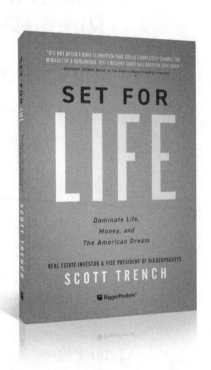

First-Time Home Buyer: The Complete Playbook to Avoiding Rookie Mistakes

Everything you need to buy your first home, from initial decisions all the way to the closing table! Scott Trench and Mindy Jensen of the *BiggerPockets Money Podcast* have been buying and selling houses for a collective thirty years. In this book, they'll give you a comprehensive overview of the home-buying process so you can consider all of your options and avoid pitfalls while jumping into the big, bad role of homeowner.

Set for Life: Dominate Life, Money, and the American Dream

Looking for a plan to achieve financial freedom in just five to ten years? *Set for Life* is a detailed fiscal plan targeted at the median-income earner starting with few or no assets. It will walk you through three stages of finance, guiding you to your first $25,000 in tangible net worth, then to your first $100,000, and then to financial freedom. *Set for Life* will teach you how to build a lifestyle, career, and investment portfolio capable of supporting financial freedom to let you live the life of your dreams.

ABOUT THE
AUTHOR

DAN SHEEKS is a high school teacher, real estate investor, and personal finance advocate in Denver, Colorado. In his eighteen years as a teacher, Dan has taught various business subjects—including financial literacy, entrepreneurship, personal finance, and marketing—and worked with thousands of students. Embedded in his classes is the co-curricular DECA club, in which students travel, compete, acquire leadership skills, do community service, and have fun! His students have competed in entrepreneurship, personal finance, marketing, and hospitality services with much success at the state and national levels over the years.

In late 2019, Dan launched the SheeksFreaks community with a simple blog website and an Instagram page. The mission was simple: Provide young people with free money advice so they could live their best lives. The SheeksFreaks community is dedicated to helping young people learn money management skills to achieve early financial independence by using specific saving methods, earning extra income, and investing. The main passions motivating Dan in his endeavors are: (1) working with young people, (2) advocating for personal finance education, (3) the early

financial independence movement, and (4) real estate investing.

Dan and his wife have various real estate investments, including multifamily, single-family, and Airbnb properties, as well as out-of-state BRRRRs. They currently have fifteen units in the Denver metro area, Colorado Springs, and Detroit (and they continue to grow their portfolio).

Dan volunteers in the MoneyWi$er initiative out of the Colorado Attorney General's Office with a few other hand-picked experts from around the state. The program strives to advance financial literacy in Colorado secondary education. He is also a contributing blog writer for BiggerPockets.

In his free time, Dan enjoys Colorado's many natural wonders through mountain biking, road biking, hiking, camping, and golfing. He lives just outside of Denver with his wife, Vanessa, and their son, Callum.

How to contact Dan:
LINKEDIN: Dan Sheeks
INSTAGRAM: @sheeksfreaks and @dsheeks
YOUTUBE: sheeksfreaks
EMAIL: dan@sheeksfreaks.com
WEBSITE: www.sheeksfreaks.com